THE THINKING BODY

Exploring the Relation of the Body to Reality, the Mind and the Socio

First published in 2018 by OrtonRoad Books

16 Salisbury Gardens

Newcastle upon Tyne, NE2 1HP, UK

ISBN 978-1-9993086-1-2

'...no one has yet determined what the body can do, that is, experience has not yet taught anyone what the body can do from the laws of Nature alone, insofar as Nature is only considered to be corporeal, and what the body can do only if it is determined by the mind. For no one has yet come to know the structure of the body so accurately that he could explain all its functions...This shows well enough that the body itself, simply from the laws of its own nature, can do many things which its mind wonders at.'

Benedict de Spinoza, *Ethics,* Part III

TABLE OF CONTENTS

PREFACE

This book has grown out of a 20 years-long friendship with Joel Yoeli. His ideas helped me understand how philosophy arises out of and returns to daily living. I've put them into some sort of shape here and added to them as an emphasis grew which neither of us foresaw. Because the ideas were discussed by word of mouth, copied during a talk or from memory afterwards or in written correspondence I have let them merge into one authorial voice. The object was always to be true to the ideas themselves. The irony is that these ideas are no secret; they are all in the public domain. But I know of no single work that spells them out in their entirety. There is something of a parallel development of these ideas in the works of a disparate group of thinkers that I identify in the Introduction. Joel's and their journeys might have overlapped but he remains unfamiliar with some of their work. In brief, what I was exposed to was not so much a set of theories as a method. It involves searching lightly and convivially (in a one-to-one conversation or group) for meta-concepts in order to bridge splits; working through and past intellectual positions, while allowing for and letting go of the grip of personality as and when it tightens. It puts a conversation at the heart of philosophy. This is a place where new thinking arises as people start to accept each other. It is public philosophy at its most vibrant.

I need to stress at the outset that there presently exists no philosophical language with which to revise the concept of mind. And yet I refer to mind over and again in later pages. It is conventionally used today as a synonym for thought. At school and college we are exhorted to develop 'a mind of your own.' I take this to be one of the blighting features of the world we live in. I define it to mean the opposite: non-thinking. Unless it is used wisely, it is an almost intractable impediment to free thought. My use of the word 'mind' in this way might appear to be counter-intuitive, bloody-minded or just wrong. I am aware that it might initially throw the reader into confusion. In the absence of such a language I can only ask the reader at the outset to 'be prepared!'

I've been immensely fortunate to make new friends in groups that met in one café or another over many years. I have to select from among them for special thanks those who nudged, queried and supported me as I ploughed through earlier drafts - Mary Whitby, Ian Patience, Leigh Rooney, Mike Boggon, Tony Ward, Mike Spencer, and of course Joel. For generally keeping me up to the mark a very warm thank-you to Jen Thomas, Janet Darbyshire, Lucian Peterca, Dennis Barker and Trevor Leonard. I owe a big debt of gratitude to my children Andrew, Judy and Penny for their sustained support, and to Andrew for his IT expertise. I greatly benefited from the clarity George Dimitri, Leigh Rooney and Ian Patience brought to issues that at one time were beginning to appear intractable - warmest thanks. I owe Anthony Morgan a debt of gratitude for letting me read his correspondence with Joel. I can only repeat to Joel, heartfelt thanks. Mary made my task immeasurably easier by giving up so many warm summer days. All mistakes, omissions and infelicities are of course my own.

INTRODUCTION

When the magnificence of the world strikes us we can respond in one of two ways. We can rest our attention lightly on it and leave it unaffected. Or, we can seek to know it. In the first case the mind is at ease, waiting for the world to present itself; in the second case it is agitated, seeking to gain knowledge of the world and thereby impose a grip on it. (I refer to 'world' hereafter to mean all, everything, universe, reality or totality, not only this planet.) This issue matters because the world is a hypothesis. Thus, questions that ask whether the world is unified or split must be held in suspension. Philosophy has nonetheless to explain the link between mind and the world because we access the latter through the former. And we do know, thanks to Kant, that mind cannot deal with things in their entirety. Indeed Kant and Hegel tell us that mind works by fragmenting or limiting. But with regard to the world as a whole, we can take up William James' argument for a 'soft' unity that incorporates all oppositions. A reasonable view, he deemed it, holds so long as no case against it is proven. It is thus more plausible to consider mind as a part of the world that is prone to split away from reality than to leap to the conclusion that the world is itself split. This is the view I take here and it leads me back to my opening remark: giving attention to the world without wanting to change it requires the use of an ability to reflect that is at ease with itself. Only in this way is it possible to philosophise and only in this way possible to quieten the clamour of mind that makes us feel we have let go of our senses; and so finally to accept that we are real. My purpose in this book is to show that the way we react to wonder crucially affects our approach to life and philosophy. I declare my allegiance straight away – I am drawn to a view of philosophy that has persisted in finding magnificence in the unity of all things from the ancients to today. This is an inclusive intellectual project that makes room for all fissiparous or antagonistic tendencies. It starts with the Greeks who by all accounts lived lives of fearless immediacy, culminating intellectually in Plato's oblique message of an *a priori* monism. They were allied with Jewish theologians in the Axial Age quest to determine what was distinctive about humankind. The medieval Jewish philosopher Maimonides interpreted this as a search for a simple absolute unity which manifests when God reaches out to people. Benedict Spinoza brought Plato's and Maimonides' insight into modern times by showing how joy arises from a sense that all things connect. Striving to develop this message in the shadow of Kant and Hegel, Franz

Rosenzweig explained what magnificence amounts to, while Martin Buber clarified what it means to have an enriching relationship with another human being. Nearer the present, Ivan Illich showed how a harmonious communal life can be organised. Then there are the thinkers from disparate intellectual backgrounds who developed systems theory and helped us to understand the fluid patterns of human interaction. The socio (of which more later) develops an idea about human interconnectivity initiated by Gilles Deleuze. Finally I include Irvin Yalom because he was able to discern philosophical import in the dynamics of groups. All but Plato, Spinoza and Deleuze of the aforementioned arguably stand outside the mainstream of philosophy. (1) I am particularly attracted to this mix of thinkers and emphases because they conceive of critical thinking and thereby philosophy as arising in the very moment of human encounter. Philosophy, they are saying, is lived rather than made objective. They converge around other themes too. For example, they took everything in the world to be connected; life to be about a readiness to hear the call of reality; philosophy to be a meeting between people; an always-already Other waits ready to puncture one's pretensions to be a self. Remarkably heterodox, often Jewish, of a continental philosophical leaning and deriving from an implicit Socratic-Platonic monism, this loose grouping has persisted as a presence on the outer edge of the canon, even though they are truly heirs of Plato and Spinoza.

I

In the following pages I draw on the ideas of the grouping mentioned above to ask four questions. One, why have particularity and theory of mind come to dominate philosophy? I will argue that modern philosophy's failure to build on the classical insight of givenness has created a fascination with mind (in the way I have defined in the Preface, as non-thinking) that has severed philosophy's connection to people at large and taken away its ability to reduce human suffering. The concepts of givenness and *a priori* point to a world that precedes our thinking about it. Moreover, what is accepted as the tool of thinking about the world – the mind – misleads us; it has become a tainted idea. When it encounters the complexity of the world it responds by perceiving dualisms. It expresses a commitment to particularity and theories of mind that predictably produce mind-body splits. Two, why turn to mind as a tool in philosophy when it is becoming clear that mind is the child of a greater force with the power to undermine freedom of thought and human wellbeing – the socio? Three, why place especial emphasis on mind when it is itself an idea that only evolved in the first place in order to understand the body? The body is part of the world; the mind is only (by now) a discredited attempt to understand it. The body is the key human connection to the world. It is material in the sense that a pebble is material; this is an issue for science. Its materiality is not an issue for philosophy, for which mind is the problem. By acting as an anchor the body moderates the mind's disposition to impose structures on thought. Mind, as Nietzsche tells us, should remember its necessary modesty and its humble place with regard to the 'formation of a superior body.' (2) Four, why has the potential of metaphysics and philosophical method to understand the ways that mind and the socio impose structures on thinking been so long neglected? To follow where mind takes us prevents us from challenging the suppositions that sustain the very concept of mind. The same is true of the socio. Philosophical method, long neglected during the ascendancy of mind, bridges dichotomies by carrying thinking to the universal. Even the seeming ubiquity of the socio, I suggest, is not beyond the reach of philosophical method.

My claim is twofold. Firstly, that philosophy seeks to discover and remove obstructions to thinking. Until we do this we do not think and thus struggle to accept that we are real. Secondly, the mind and the socio are the very obstructions that make it impossible for us to recognise that we are real. They persuade us that we are thinking when we are not. Philosophy cannot be concerned with discovering reality while it is embroiled with the mind and the socio. When we appreciate the classical insight that reality is a given, we see that reality is not an object to be reached or connected to, as if it is 'out there.' It is an always-already state in which we inhere. Philosophy arises when we use our capability to think about this state, and then to continue further by thinking about our thinking. Philosophy helps us to make sense of things – issues in daily life; strong feelings like love, hate and fear - in these ways. (3) It does this by helping us avoid falling into the dichotomising disposition of the mind. It comes as no surprise that attacks on the notion of givenness start from an acceptance that mind is to be relied upon. (4) Only philosophical method, I suggest, has the power fully to demolish obstructions to our understanding, and, as yet, it awaits practitioners who will take up the baton presently carried by AW Moore. (5) The requisite first step is to recognise the unity of the world. Heraclitus spelled out the rudiments near the dawn of philosophy. He explained how things come to be by arguing that reason presents nature in two aspects, the visible and invisible, both of which are seeking unity. Opposites are not in conflict; they are linked by common ground. There is thus an emergent monism in all oppositions. Furthermore, as Gilbert Ryle reminded us with regard to the body-mind issue, when we talk about a person's mind we are not talking of an entity distinct from the body. This is not to deny that dualisms are a commonplace in public and private discourse. But they indicate a cessation of thinking and the adoption of a position. The limitlessness of the world allows for all possible splits, fractures, oppositions, limitations and cessations to be included without the world itself becoming split.

A second question then arises: how does the unity of the world manifest in life? One response to this question is Emmanuel Levinas' idea of the Other. The Other constitutes me as a subject; it stands in for all reality. This idea enables a form of subjectivity to be sustained. But I take the question to mean more than this: that the observing mind can be shown to be redundant. It is as a response to this question that the human body is being 'rediscovered' as a microcosm that replicates the macrocosm of the world. The task of philosophy, I take it, is to return the mind to the body whence, as a thought-experiment, it was 'detached' 2500 years ago. Only after we have completed this move can we fully return the body to the world where its position vis-à-vis other beings can be situated. I will argue in later pages that distress occurs when our thinking is dualist (non-thinking in my terms), and further that the latter arises when thinking is said to dissociate from the body. Presently we mistakenly treat mind as if it is an out-of-the-body faculty with which we somehow mysteriously connect. The dualist and materialist origins of neuroscience determine that it goes further and locates mind in a single bodily organ, the brain.(6) The monism for which Spinoza cogently argued has come down intact to our times. But it is still a small voice crowded out by vociferous supporters of particularisation and theories of mind. Recognition of the central place of the body in mainstream philosophical discourse today derives primarily from the work of Gilles Deleuze and Maurice Merleau-Ponty. But Deleuze's remark, 'Not that the body thinks…' represents the ultimate position of both. (7) Is this the final word? The purpose of this book is to present a thorough-going case for a thinking body.

The dualism that underlies German idealism and analytic philosophy and the relativism that is expressed in postmodernism have meant that resolution of the body-mind dilemma has most recently been consigned to art, aesthetic styles of living, or the cognitive sciences. It is little wonder that human relationship is prone to excitation and agitation and to arguments that lead to lose-lose situations, and that philosophy is widely perceived to be detached from matters of public concern other than morality and politics. Marx's spectre of alienation pales in comparison. Indeed, the failure to appreciate the implications of the way we misunderstand mind requires a major re-assessment of the intellectual canon. Only when the mind is anchored in the body and is no longer able to constrict thought can we abandon the illusion that we are agents of our own thoughts. A claim to possess a mind of one's own tells us that our thinking is structured and ordered and at variance with the indefinability of reality. This is because mind is a concept that depicts a defensive, reactive response to a fear of the unknown. It fears the unpredictability of thought. No wonder; thought connects us to untold forces in the world. So, an urgent need exists to drop the concept of mind altogether. Only then can we recognise the way thinking helps us to make sense of things. Thinking may turn out to be the biggest connection of the body to the world, but it is only one player in the microcosmic universe that is the body, a holographic idea of the world a la Leibniz. The body is variously connected to the world: the nervous and immune systems vie with thinking in this regard.

Philosophical preoccupation with a mind-body split becomes superfluous once we appreciate how the mind blocks thought. Once thought is released from the grip of mind there is no split at all, for reflective thought occurs within the body as within the world. The body thinks only in the sense that it can tap the capacity of the world to reflect. Mind or non-thinking blocks thinking when a sense of self grows. Thought then becomes rule-bound and withers. This issue will be taken up in Chapters Eight and Nine. In a proper sense it is the world that thinks, and it is this force that operates within the body.

It is only after we have addressed the issue of mind however that we realise there exists a second threat to our freedom. Behind mind, it is now becoming clear, is an insidious force I call the socio. It has such presence that it passes for an alternative world with greater power to control our lives than the mind. The first step towards understanding the socio is for human beings to let go of opinions or intellectual positions; we are back at my first point now – allowing the body to utilise the capacity of the world to think. Thought is a force that connects us to all of reality; it is not concerned to systemise or organise our relation to the world.

Indeed, when the body acts as a receptacle, conduit or transmitter it lets the world call out to us. It is a big move to contemplate the possibility that we do not have a mind of our own and that 'our' thoughts are already integral to the world with which we are striving to connect. It might be claimed that philosophy's task is complete once human beings attain unmediated connection to reality. But what if an alternative world has already supervened; one that our struggles with mind obscures? Is philosophy up to the further task of understanding this force? At this juncture we must call on metaphysics and philosophical method. Obscured hitherto by an emphasis on epistemology and subjectivity within the philosophical canon they nonetheless possess a potential to help us understand how our connection with others and the world can become clean and immediate. The working out of these issues is nothing less than a category step in philosophy.

II

Philosophy has rarely operated from a sense of *a priori* wholeness or totality. It always seems to be teetering on the edge of becoming an adjunct of the sub-discipline of theory of mind. Today's thinking owes a debt to Kant for demonstrating that the world can only be accessed as a personal experience. Kant questioned the use of reason as a tool with which to access the world. Kant was merely pointing out something obvious - reason is only one part of reality; it cannot address totality entire. The Greeks, used reason differently: for them it was a practical tool with which to clear away the debris from *their own minds,* debris that stopped them being revealed as already real. Nonetheless, the use of parts of totality to express or explain the whole a la Kant has become a common philosophical practise. It may be no surprise then that the public reputation of philosophy is accused of an overweening deference to mind. It seems almost impossible to move from a path laid down by Kant, a mind-dominated path strewn with dichotomies and limitations, reflecting a world segmented into portions and parts. As Deleuze put it in the 1970s, '…'today [we live] in an age of partial objects, bricks that have been broken to bits, and leftovers…We no longer believe in a primordial totality that once existed or in a final totality that awaits us at some future date.' (8) Like earlier thinkers who glimpsed primordial wholeness we are paying a heavy price. The rectitude the Greeks associated with the god Apollo seems impossible to dislodge. Socrates was condemned; others too, like Spinoza. Schopenhauer was depressed, Nietzsche verged on madness, Wagner and Heidegger turned to fascism. Wittgenstein believed that philosophising amounts to a state of madness in which all sense of fixity begins to evaporate. In a narcissistic, mind-besotted world that is hungry for knowledge it seems a step too far to ask us to turn things around and, rather than burnish the idea of a personal mind, instead to give primacy to the world. Yet, thinking bodies have this capacity, as I intend to demonstrate. Put another way, philosophy can be conceived of as a cry for a feminised version of men to appear, akin to Oedipus in old age – accepting, reflective, lacking all illusion, in a word, wise. Such a move Spinoza tells us starts when we contemplate things under the aspect of eternity. Are we able to conceive of a state of affairs in which there are no dogmatic opinions, disagreements or storms in teacups, no God or Fall and thus no need for redemption? One route is to enter therapy; but another is to conceive of such a thing.

It might however be felt that the opportunity to resolve these issues has passed, that Apollonian order long ago hijacked the exuberant, undefined and fearsome energy of the god Dionysus. Yet from Heraclitus onwards thinkers have been reminding us that life is raw, that flux is the only certainty and that, when we let go, it throws us into a 'vertigo of immanence,' as Deleuze put it. Plato and his predecessors offered a way to avoid paralysis. They accepted the world as the only referent that can reliably be turned to, meanwhile chipping away at the blockages to their thinking that prevented them recognising the reality of everything. As a result they were said to engage fearlessly with the world. Since those times the world has suffered millennia of dominance by socio-backed mind. Bodies have been seen as inferior to mental powers. Occasionally a thinker like Rosenzweig or Heidegger has rebelled, telling us of a time before logos appeared, of a time when thought and nature were one. Indeed Spinoza went so far as to bring thought and body into relation with each other. Our task now, it is becoming clear, is to draw out the implications of the relation between the body and the world.

These points are taken up below. Because the greatest challenge facing philosophy thus far has been the relation of mind to reality, this is the focus of Chapters One to Seven. Section One looks at what it means to say that reality is everything there is; it brings discourse about the body alongside that about reality by treating the body as a microcosm of the world. Section Two looks at the way a belief has become entrenched in philosophy suggesting that the mind has an independent status. This Section then examines the way that claims about the primacy of mind have entered the philosophical canon and weakened it from within. Section Three introduces the idea of the socio, a force not merely bigger than mind but one that suffuses mind, negating it as a force capable of working towards human freedom. Section Four affirms the ability of a re-invigorated philosophy to reconnect us to reality. It explains the body as a monad-like manifestation of the world, meanwhile pointing to ways that such a development might play out in our lives.

CHAPTER ONE - PHILOSOPHY

GENERAL

Philosophy seeks to free thought from all constraints. But, as simple as this objective might sound, it covers a complexity of moves that need to be explored. I start with the hypothesis that in the beginning the world contained everything without form and as yet unrealised or revealed, including thought. (1) Then, at some point, the universe began to reflect upon itself. By looking back to where it arose, thought brought the world into being. This is the Platonic message – thought conceived the world. Innumerable questions arise at this juncture. If philosophy has a 'job' to do, is it to return us to that prior state? Or is it to move thinking forward to a state of as-yet unrealised completion? Are the world and life already in a state of harmony and the talk of split a misunderstanding of the place of philosophy? Or is the world itself ruptured? These questions resonate in our lives daily, whether or not we articulate them in this form. However, the articulation of these thoughts seems to run up against unseen barriers. When human beings emerged from the swamp or the savannah they appear to have become suspicious of each other. Could the cause have been that, as thinking becomes freer it seems to bring chaos in its wake? It is not clear. Nonetheless, an early response to this suspicion was to corral thinking. Thought withered as it became both personal (when we say 'I have a mind of my own') and rule-bound. I distinguish mind (or non-thinking) as a set of rules and structures from thought as a force within the world. So, put another way, thinking disappeared under the impress of mind. Moreover, mind now developed a sense of its own capacity; it began to act as if it were independent of the body through which it expressed itself. An adherence to the concept of mind arose, starting in the Axial Age (800-200BC) and expounded definitively by Descartes. This was expressed as a belief that body and thought operate separately from each other. Mind came to be accepted unquestioningly as the true perceiver of reality. The suggestion we must address is that at some point human beings were fully exposed to reality and, instead of drawing on the reflective capacity of the world, they instead immediately became over-exposed to mind-creations. If we accept this suggestion the question then arises: can we return to the earlier realm?

Plato argued for a return of thought to the body in order to free it. How this can be done is explained at length in later chapters. But we need first to take a look at thought. It is a special case, being a force that connects us with a lost primordial world. Reality doesn't knock on our door; rather, thought sets reality free. We cannot conceive of the world without thought. Yet thought unsettles as it moves – towards mysticism for example. It thinks about itself and, at the same time, it includes that which does the thinking. The world now opens up to the notion of reality in terms such as 'cosmos' or 'universe.' People appear always to have had a sense that their self-conscious sense of totality is a tiny fragment of the world, as revealed in myths. Thought is capable of speculation and of releasing new thoughts. It does this by inserting itself between mind and the world; here it begins to chip away at the human reliance on rule-bound mind, boring ever larger holes in its carapace. In Platonic terms, it reveals that reality is more than mere shadows on the wall of a mind-created cave; rather it lurks beyond mind, awaiting our full engagement.

This book is a call for philosophy to be appreciated as the only means with which to leave Plato's Cave. However, philosophy's traditional attempt to free people from obstacles and encumbrances that stymie a thorough-going immersion in reality has always been under threat. Nietzsche talks of the world being divided into two forces – the order, beauty and reassurance that he associated with the Greek god Apollo and the flux, uncertainty and unpredictability he associated with the god Dionysus. Apollonian forces of order, Nietzsche is saying, always tend to impose themselves on Dionysian forces of immanence. I am saying that mind operates through Apollonian forces. The process is simple – it starts when the complex structures and injunctions that we call the mind impose themselves on thinking. The all-conquering mind, now virtually an autonomous force, then appears to separate itself from the body. The mind uses the idea of self as a vehicle to force people to adopt an onerous sense of personal responsibility, with a concomitant burden of blame and guilt. This occurs because rules are unable to cope with flux; the mind inevitably misreads the world. Philosophy offers to rectify this situation by interposing itself between the mind and the sentient being, thus bypassing the mind as thinking returns to the body. The agitation that imposed rules upon thinking gives way again to simplicity and calmness. This can be expressed as a return of human beings to a primordial place of acceptance and connectivity. Simplicity is a state of openness to reality. It allows us to avoid mistaking our mental (in)disposition for reality itself.

METHOD

'First philosophy' or metaphysics, which has been neglected in recent times, is philosophy's way of addressing the challenges we face as we strive to make sense of things. AW Moore expresses it thus: 'To whatever extent the unexamined life is not worth living, neither is the life without metaphysics.' (2) However, the success of postmodernism in reducing grand narratives to rubble has left us with only a fractured world to contemplate. I take this to be the result of a misreading of the place of mind in philosophy that has found its way virtually unchallenged to the very heart of the canon. Spinoza is the signal exception. Philosophers fail when they are seduced by mind. When they succumb they lose touch with wholeness. The result is evident: the canon abounds in dualisms. Wherever one looks, moreover, the separate branches of philosophy claim to speak with the authority of, and without reference to, the whole. Rarely is a context or remit offered up that is large enough to embrace or underpin philosophy entire. This may have something to do with a tendency of even the greatest thinkers to make a dash to be recognised by posterity. They ignore Socrates' insight that philosophy is a never-ending questioning of positions. Writing struggles to handle the fluidity and lack of directionality of open-ended face-to-face questioning. Plato got round this problem by writing in dialogic form and playfully opening up the text to elisions and tangential references, possibly to use as a provocative teaching resource. Adherence to mind also reveals itself when thinkers seek an outcome rather than find new questions in the old ones. Positions arise when the mind becomes fascinated with itself; it acts as if it has split away from reality. It even acts as if its internal operations are unconnected. Then it notices its internal dissonances, panics and seeks reassurance and definition.

However, philosophy will not go along with the moves of mind. Instead, it seeks the origin of things; it takes us back to primordial thingness. It appeared first among the Pre-Socratics who located everything in nature. Modern philosophy has since abandoned this search, to the chagrin of Nietzsche and Heidegger. Nonetheless, philosophy then proclaimed that God was dead and affirmed that everything lay inside the world. Coincidentally, two other equally momentous things happened. Firstly, the rise of philosophy promised to stop mind from masquerading as thinking. Secondly, thinking was now free to engage with reality. Before I open up this sentence, which is ripe with implications for all that appears in the following pages, I must first stress that all I am saying about mind and reality applies only to the practice of philosophy. The probability that relatively few people at any one moment practised philosophy rigorously does not detract from my claim that philosophy cleared the way for thinking to blossom and for everything to be in the world. For those people who thought in the sense I mean here God could never be reborn again other than as an idea; and mind was relegated to an irritating nuisance, never to corrupt thought again, despite a general unawareness of these developments. But I want to return to the distinction I am making between thinking and mind, with all that it conveys for philosophy. I will take thinking first.

Thinking equates to living; this is because thinking is a manifestation of reality - we are directly immersed in reality when we think. Thought is neither a thing nor a construct; it is a manifestation of reality anchored in the body. Because it is not a thing it is not possible to describe what it *is*. But by a process of elimination, we can say what it is *not*. It is not content, structure, pattern or purpose, all of which arise from mind. In short, thinking is a meta-process that takes us beyond partiality or attribution. Put otherwise, only 'thinking about thinking' – the usual definition of philosophy - is thinking. It cannot be repeated often enough that only philosophical thinking will reconnect us to reality. Another way to approach thinking is to say that the key issue is *that we are thinking* not, crucially, *how* we think or *what* we think about. It is not concerned with outcomes. The reason these distinctions cannot be overemphasised is that, over the ages, philosophy as generally been concerned with how we think or what we think about, with the result that thinkers have failed to appreciate that everything they wrote is determinedly dualist. When free of the shackles and impositions that go with a dualistic approach however, thinking relates to reality without mediation. The key function of philosophy is to free thought and thereby free living so that life becomes nothing less than magnificent.

Now, to turn to the mind: this is something entirely different. Mind is an intellectual construct which, in human beings, constrains thinking. It is non-thinking. It is a way of imposing order on thinking by forcing it to partake of the structures and partialities mentioned above. It is orderly Apollo reacting against the maddening chaos of Dionysus. As thinking begins to flourish it generates a counter-movement that is fearful of the indefinable consequences of the first impulse. The counter-movement is what I call mind. It fears lack of definition and shies away from the vitality which can infuse immanence and process. Moreover, mind is powerfully interconnected with society. Both resist Dionysian flux. Philosophy's ability to free thinking from the constraints of mind allows mind to become porous; it becomes a receptacle into which reality can begin to seep. It has returned to its place of origin as an adjunct to thinking. But this is true only when the mind is assiduously cultivated by philosophical practice. The fact that the regressive nature of mind is positively encouraged by society right down to today has demanded of anyone who seeks to philosophise that they rein in mind by anchoring it in the body.

Philosophy's ability to do this is unrelentingly powerful. This is because philosophy is more than the march of ideas, such as the Enlightenment, French Revolution, and so on. It goes ever deeper as it searches for what is permanent and irreducible. It seeks to set the ship of life afloat on an already-present sea of reality. In the process it has to brush aside the Veil of Maya that obscures truth. Conformist and oppressive thoughts are acquired in the process of accommodating to the authority of parents, siblings, school and so on. The reining in of mind amounts to the rediscovering of one's natural place in the universe. At the heart of philosophy lies recognition that the deed has already been done, that there is no escaping it. It thus takes something exceptional for philosophising to begin. Slavoj Zizek described philosophy as arising in acts of madness. But philosophy makes light of such descriptions by taking us deep into the realm of enchantment, risk-taking and magnificence, of living without a care in the world once we are prepared, as Nietzsche almost enjoined us, to live without boundaries. 'A life in which the gods are not invited isn't worth living,' is Roberto Calasso's play on Socrates' famous sentiment. (3) This is a life of splendour. The questions philosophy asks are carved out of the lived life, but the possibilities it reveals are Olympian. Cognisant of failed relationships, enmity, bitterness, ennui and wars which may be said to result from a misrecognition of reality, philosophy reminds us that we are already partaking in reality. Because reality is everything there is, it includes everything that ever arose and might yet arise; even a conception of the world as irretrievably split between mind and reality or a rejection of reality itself is included. For example, connectedness is not an historical event or developmental stage but an eternal occurrence. Human beings have but temporarily lost the memory of it. The search for the origin of things - the source of movement, vitality or potential - is concerned only to apprehend things, not to change them. The world is magnificent already. Philosophy seeks that which is mysterious, wonderful and magnificent because it includes the as yet unknown. Moreover, by constantly reshuffling the cards, it includes that which turns life into a different kind of riddle. Undoubtedly, those who stay the course might feel crazy once fixed positions become no longer tenable. But this helter-skelter journey is what a philosopher chooses.

It is not uncommon to hear mind described as the way forward for the human race. One of the major claims I make here is that, far from being a way forward, mind is the problem. It has been a formidable one, but it is only an idea, and we are capable of abandoning it. Mind is a set of structures and channels whose rigidity causes thinking to be shallow, reductive, dichotomous and agitated. Whereas thinking, free of mind, is a simple, calm and mundane activity that flows within the complex processes and connectedness of the body. The point can be expressed in this way – I open my eyes in the morning and let reality in. I think about the world; that is to say I rest my thoughts on it without seeking to analyse or change it. Yet, very quickly, structures start to impinge on my apprehension; mind moves into operation. A sense of self emerges and becomes concrete, and my first apprehension or impulse withers under a barrage of self-doubt and anxiety about what is real. The initial, unmediated apprehension of the world is succeeded by the imposition of rules that constrain thinking and engender uncertainty and acts of bad faith. One loses a sense of being one's true self.

An injunction that runs throughout this book is: dispense with the mind (non-thinking)! Philosophy is not concerned with the actions of the mind except insofar as they are an impediment to attaining reality. Mind is unfree, subject to feed-back loops and able to encounter and confuse itself. Thus philosophy has to use it with the greatest circumspection. And, irony of ironies, philosophy uses mind as its main tool to free thinking from the grip of mind! Accordingly philosophy has to question itself unceasingly; it does this by using mind to scrutinise the assumptions made by the mind itself. Philosophising demands exceptional courage and commitment, as can be adduced in the works of Ludwig Wittgenstein, Gilles Deleuze and Slavoj Zizek. They have pointed to it as a psychotic activity in which one engages with the world with a mind increasingly opened up and thus unprotected by defences. One becomes a hostage to all the terrors and incipient madness we fear and project onto reality. This is why philosophers put philosophy above love, desire, partner, family, friends, esteem, acclaim and fortune. Free of mind they can throw themselves into what might turn out to be the maelstrom of reality. Such are the implications of adopting practises that aim to free thought by dispensing with the mind.

Philosophy never stops asking: are we built in to reality or are we an add-on? It seeks the most comprehensive response to questions. It can be accused of abstraction, but it is more than this. It is genuinely concerned with human suffering and takes it that this is caused by our inability to make sense of things. Philosophy is wholly about the lived life; it only slips away from this into issues of knowledge and epistemology when mind struggles to apprehend the way that life evolves. Such struggles arise from agitation. Mind can do many things by following logical rules or by refined guesswork. But mind divides. It is a dangerous tool, the critical use of which needs cultivating. Philosophy may be said to stand between reality on the one hand and the distorting workings of the mind on the other. In other words, philosophy enables us to think harmoniously and clearly, free of excitation and convulsion, undisturbed by dichotomous and oppositional thinking. We might conjecture that at some point critical thinking will have so penetrated the obscurities and obstacles that mind throws up that mind will no longer be needed. Or, put another way, thoroughgoing thinking will at that point only just have begun. We can assume therefore that the present unexamined practices that so often pass for thinking have never yet allowed us to think. To the extent that the philosopher-to-be accepts these comments he or she is faced with a choice – carry on living according to conventional thinking and the ways of the world or, by cultivating the mind so that it is less of an obstruction, let go of all that has hitherto been understood as 'oneself' and, kicking and screaming, enter on a never-ending metamorphosis. This conviction is the starting point of this book. It arose in response to the calls for alleviation of distress that abound in society on the one hand and the remoteness of citation-bound scholarship on the other. Philosophy has always been totally responsive to the human condition. It removes distress by showing what happens when we put the part (mind) before the whole (universe). This move leads to a belief in separation and results in a feeling of loneliness. To submit to the uncritical operation of mind is to live in a perceived opposition between parts of the whole – between the universe and the 'I,' between my fellows and the 'I,' and between elements within me such as body and mind.

The underlying method of philosophy is an unrelenting scepticism. Nothing is left unquestioned, including philosophy itself. It is like a snake eating its tail. Philosophical thinking is different from the under-powered general usage of the word 'thinking.' It critiques all concepts, statements and positions. Its practice requires fierce dedication in order to withstand all social pressures and influences. It is a much higher order of things than (self)awareness which is too generalised and restricted by structures of mind.

Philosophy moves to unity by falsifying dichotomies. It does this as much by what it doesn't say as by what it does: the best example is Socrates' use of irony. It stands contemporary values on their head by regarding the ability to doubt as more appropriate than to assert or to take a position. This doesn't mean it slips helter-skelter beyond scepticism into nihilism, or that it claims there is nothing to say. Descartes starts with doubt and then integrates his doubt into his thought; thus thought is enabled to overcome itself. In so doing the object of investigation is strengthened and the observer removed. Until the point is reached where mind can be abandoned, mind has to be managed rigorously.

Philosophy posits the world as immediately accessible; nothing is hidden or lying beyond the immediate; there is no hereafter, no afterlife. Nothing is needed to make life more amenable or less stark or to cushion one from the rawness of reality. This is expressed in the difference between the phrases *That it is* and *What it is*. The former says everything is already and always here, that if something lies unrevealed to the eye it is because the observer has not yet looked. The observer is secondary to the object of observation. The object was there in any case. The Greeks characterised this situation by describing a sculptor chipping away at a block of marble in which the sculpture lay latent, waiting to be revealed. The idea that the sculpture eventually arose from the genius of the sculptor was deemed to be overly human-centred. The latter phrase asks what a thing is as if its presence is accounted for by the fact that the observer has cast an eye on it, as if it was not there already before it was perceived. The emphasis in the latter phrase is on the agency of the observer.

The old philosophical questions (What is? How do we know? How do we live a good life?) have been answered to general satisfaction. Could it be nonetheless that philosophy has missed the point; that there is something in philosophical thinking itself that is the problem? New, bigger and more puzzling questions are now replacing the old ones as subterranean forces, previously undetected, emerge. Why, they ask, after 2500 years of philosophical enquiry, do so many people feel unfree, vulnerable or traumatised? (4) I will discuss these questions by focusing on the body in Chapter Three and on the socio in Chapter Eight. This is the next great task of philosophy. But first the knots in present thinking need investigating and undoing.

GOING ASTRAY

The dysfunctionality of mainstream philosophy is clearly evident. Sisyphus's energy may be required to turn it around. It has become a self-enclosed, internally-referencing history of ideas. Even the great philosophers at some point gave up the perpetual quest to question everything, and settled instead on a position that we now associate with their name. This is philosophy as doctrine, not as process. In the end we are offered simulacra. (5) Yet the origin and momentum of philosophy promise a transformative effect that arises in the very process of *philosophising.* In a sense Plato's *Symposium* is telling us that philosophising is the only lever we possess to make true connection to reality. All branches of philosophy are an invitation to be real, so long as none claims to replace reality. This is because metaphysics underpins all – ethics, aesthetics, epistemology, logic and knowledge. Reality lies undiscovered and is forever awaiting revelation.

Problems started at the outset when Socrates put the individual at the centre of philosophy. But Plato makes plain that Socrates' move disguises a loss of nerve, a failure to anchor his project in metaphysics. Plato reveals an understanding of something in Socrates' move that will be described later as the socio, something that blurs the relationship between individuals, a pervasive force that has dogged the history of philosophy throughout. From the beginning personhood has served as a front; it is a quick step from this concept to a belief in agency, personal responsibility, culpability and blame. What lies behind Socrates' move is however much more interesting. 'The unexamined life is not worth living' is not a reference to the individual life but to the act of confining a life solely to what is apparent. A world circumscribed by superficialities - seeking conclusions, believing in a Fall and then redemption from it – this is the life not worth living. The Greeks held that reality is eternal, a given that precedes our thinking about it, and that the subjective viewpoint is the fickle variable in an unchanging world. Things are forever as they are and the only issue is that we accept this: Oedipus' destiny. But first we must challenge the 'certainty' of the way we see things. For example, fighting for a cause, however liberal, puts the fighter in the same camp – staying on one side of a divide – as the 'bad' guy. The philosopher-to-be has a choice: one route leads to fighting for a cause, taking up societal values, or entering therapy; the other is to conceive of wholeness as seen under the aspect of eternity. Psychology claims that relationships bring about personal wholeness. But philosophy looks further than claims to subjective salvation and asks: what is relationship itself? The question pushes the mind down a rabbit hole where definitions of relationship become confused and meaningless. The mind starts out seeking conclusion, resolution or assurance and finally anchors itself in reality.

It is a matter of little wonder that, when people seek to ground their lives in something infinitely greater than themselves, they rarely seem to turn to philosophy. Succour has at different times been sought in nature and culture. Yet these concepts cannot underpin totality, Taking nature first, we can ask if it possible to speak of human nature or, for that matter any nature, as lying at the core of all behaviours, workings of the mind or social phenomena. Evolutionary psychology has undertaken to do just that, yet there is clearly too much learning, environmental culture, feedback loops, interactions and inter-relatedness to render nature absolute as a foundational philosophical concept. Perhaps culture is a worthwhile contender? Are we not, after all, the product of our culture? Isn't multi-culturalism a welcome recognition of the firm grip of respective cultures, of their enduring power and of their ontological status? Aren't we seeing a renaissance or flourishing of such an array of cultures – from sexual culture to identity culture, from food culture to habitat culture, from drug culture to etiquette? Indeed, isn't culture the hallmark of everything? As tempting as all these proposals might be, we will do well to remember Socrates' warning about the flimsy nature of culture. It makes irrational, shallow and contradictory claims, possesses no independent thinking to check against and is blindly determinist. Furthermore, cultures are proliferating to the point of fragmentation. Culture cannot speak for itself let alone for all else. Lastly, it has no claim to totality; it only has a sense of itself. Thus, nature and culture fall back, potentially leaving the field to reality.

But still people look elsewhere, for example to the professions. Yet, professionals can at best only offer a partial repair job, because they deal in knowledge that is split from the whole of life. Or, people have turned to religion which puts the nexus of reality outside us. Moreover, there has been a blossoming of self-help therapies and meditative practices outside mainstream professions in the last half-century. By default psychology has largely been left to carry the can. The problem is not lost on popular culture which is replete with references to alternative universes and forms of mind-control of whole populations.

If these forms of help can be accused of being uneven, they at least go where mainstream philosophy fears to tread.

As a parody of the way Socrates' circle connected up all aspects of personal life, mind and reality philosophy has become self-enclosed and internally-referencing. (6) No major thinker has been totally inured to the mind's siren call. This can be seen in the way that all major thinkers in the end offer a series of aborted breakthroughs that converge on the mean. A complex system of cross-referencing telegraphs where new departures will arise. Everything is kept inside established bounds. This feature thrusts on the reader the obligation to be utterly vigilant and to read between the lines of what is written. This is an appropriate response, one might think, if one were addressing playful Socratic irony that aims to convey more than can the literal text, But it is also a cautionary move when one is reading what amounts to the imposition of a closure on thinking in order to help a great mind offer their opus for publication. Because these features of the canon are barely examined it has become an exercise in theory-building and in mind-thinking-about-mind, an internal conversation between peers, comfortable, self-sustaining and closed off from the only thing that matters - being real. This may explain why the ability of philosophical method to engage with reality is not significantly drawn upon nowadays. It is difficult to see any other than a glaring disconnection between philosophy and daily life, other than the more accessible, aphorismic forms of philosophy of consolation.

Because the philosophical canon exhibits a tight form of programmatic thinking we are forced to question its value as an aid. It emphasises a narrow range of themes, such as epistemology, subjectivity and ethics, is positively addicted to dualism, and reproduces a pattern of question and answer that entrenches certain ideas and approaches. Subjectivity is a case in point: it is the result of focusing on the operation of mind rather than on mind as a tool to take thinking to the universal. We are familiar with the pattern: the desire to topple a predecessor has led to the focus on variations of the same theme. For example, Aristotle reacted against Plato's Forms and evolved his own position with regard to materialism and the excluded middle; the Neo-Platonists reacted against Aristotle and produced the One, and so on. This pattern has turned the canon into a series of positions which resist the free flow of heterodox thinking. There is a sense of self-fulfilment over time. Truly, philosophy becomes a footnote to Plato because we are guided to see things in this way. But does this do justice to thinking? This constant refinement and competition between positions that runs through the canon explains to a large degree why dualism has been able to exert its grip for so long.

It must be said at this point that this book stands outside the philosophy canon whilst acknowledging and delving into all that constitutes it. Although philosophers rightly stand on the shoulders of earlier giants, philosophy nonetheless needs to be aware of its own centripetal tendencies. A view from outside is thus warranted in order to pinpoint assumptions that permeate the canon as a whole and still go unchallenged. Here I bring reality, thinking, mind, body and the socio into the orbit of that challenge.

RETURN TO THE UNIVERSAL

So, to return to the main theme of this chapter: philosophy asks us to free ourselves of anything that would obstruct an unmediated acceptance of the world. This means working towards removing the imprint of personality, culture, psychology, personal history and narrative in order to become a Socrates, knowing that we know nothing. It means becoming a vessel or receptacle for the world to pass through, emptied out so that, in the entering and passing through, nothing is changed but more is acknowledged. What we are apprehending is then not the workings of our mind but reality itself.

Untrammelled thinking occurs, unthreatened by the extreme states of excitation or depression, relaxed and able to apprehend the world without changing it in a search for knowledge, free of the anxiety and mind-fragmentation that we mistake for the world itself.

Philosophising on the other hand need not be arduous. It remains a simple, uncomplicated process of being in the world that reveals thinking as a manifestation of reality. This is to say that critical thinking allows us to live simply and living simply opens up our relation to others (how else could it be other?); and that, in discussions that are mostly free of entrenched positions, engagements will grow that nurture human wellbeing. On any account, to engage with others philosophically requires one to be calm, grounded, relaxed, congruent and receptive. This is so that one's thinking does not for long solidify into a position and one's relationship to others does not for long become oppositional. The infamous case of Wittgenstein's Poker – where Wittgenstein is supposed to have wielded a poker in a fit of pique following remarks made by Karl Popper – shows where philosophical opposition can take us. In these states unity arises in the process of genuine intellectual engagement. Inevitably, solidifying will occur at some point; then the role of philosophising becomes one of releasing thinking from its frozen state, continuing again and again as later positions are mounted. It has often been said that sustained friendships are nurtured when friends keep their minds open to the wonder of each other. The importance of philosophising in this way cannot be understated: it lay at the heart of Socrates' philosophy project. Only when one is open-minded and receptive to the other is one able to fill the Socratic role of receiver, container and questioner.

SECTION ONE: REALITY AND THE BODY

CHAPTER TWO - REALITY IS ALL THERE IS

We can now look more closely at the issues raised in the Introduction, starting with the anchor for everything else - reality. Reality is a hypothesis: we can't get there. The statement 'reality is all there is' defines its irreducibility to anything else. Reality thus gains ontological status in terms of the thingness of life. This is what Heidegger and Wittgenstein meant by the phrase '*that it is,*' to distinguish it from the concern of epistemology with '*what it is.*' At the outset thinking about reality is a process of mind engaging with mind; we think about our thinking about reality. This very process starts to bang heads together and sparks might begin to fly as a side-effect of the philosophical process.

Yet, by general observation, it seems that the idea or prospect of fully entering reality horrifies us, as is revealed by myriad attempts to escape it. We resort to many ideas to tame reality – fate, art, will, ethics for instance. Slavoj Zizek tells us that reality abides only in representation since Kant. There is something about the idea of totality that seems impossible to live with, something so painful or effortful that it is deemed undesirable. Maybe, as Foucault claimed, the Greeks saw themselves as manifestations of reality where instead today we struggle because we conceive of ourselves as the centre of the universe. We let reality into our lives only in the guise of the other. The Greeks accepted reality as always, already here, in Heidegger's words, so that one's thinking already constitutes a second move within the 'all' of reality. The Greek stance is accepted in this book: I look out at the world and think about everything beyond my mind as reality, but a reality *that includes me and my mind within it*. I am not the centre of the universe, nor am I detached from it. There is no horror in this position. Perhaps horror arises when I see reality as beginning beyond my mind, one I am detached from. In Foucault's terms, reality has today been allocated the status of knowledge, and has slipped out of the realm of ontology into that of epistemology. Of course reality as a concept is open to questioning. Defining its magnitude is impossible however; indeed, attempts to do so can sound platitudinous. But some things can definitely be said. Reality goes far beyond the fleeting nature of mere human preoccupations, making a Caesar or Napoleon someone whose 'achievements' are wiped out of the sand by the next gust of wind. Reality, Bergson makes clear, is a joining-up of particularities that sustains eternity in every moment. The magnitude of philosophical thinking allows it to rise to the challenge of reality. Such an engagement has been expressed in terms of the power of the divine.

I

The nature of the phrases we use is crucial. Take the phrase: reality is everything there is. The 'everything' is straightforward, as separately is the verb to be, 'is.' However, once we combine them strange things start to happen: the relation between them becomes problematic. This is what philosophy does – it forces thought on us. It throws at us a phrase that contains a contradiction which pushes us beyond our usual limits as we think about it. We can't escape it. We do not have a straightforward answer and are made to realise, for example, that Aristotle's idea of an excluded middle will not hold. Now we have to face the possibility that A can be B at the same time as being separate from it. Whitehead's idea of 'process philosophy' comes into play by introducing conundrums or ideas that require us to unravel things further, rather than offer a quick answer. Philosophy operates by telling us there is a margin between where our present thinking has taken us and where the philosophical process might take us. Reality is not a known; it is not there to fit into our criteria. We must change our own thinking by conceptualising in order to accept reality. In this way we transcend ourselves.

What can be said about reality that is viable? We have to start with the idea of totality, before we go into distinctions. The boldness of the claim that a concept can carry *all* in its wake elevates it from being a passing thought to being a philosophical concept. This can sustain it against the effect of afterthought, which in most people prevents philosophical thinking. The idea of reality therefore equates with infinity, eternity, indeterminacy, potentiality, extra-body experience, and stochastic processes. It brings concepts such as the divine and the mystical into discourse. It postulates multiverse possibilities (even if string theory ultimately proves untenable). In short, it invites us to philosophise rather than to apply the specialised thinking of science, logic, politics, psychology, sociology, or any other form that anthropomorphises or segments philosophy. Reality *is all there is:* this is so obvious that it is really a tautology. Yet, it is arguably the most fundamental of concepts. Had virtue not been Socrates' main concern, reality would surely have sat atop the Forms or Ideas in the Platonic edifice instead of the Good. Philosophy is the ultimate test of thought. That is to say, in the way that the virtue of Good stands at the head of Plato's hierarchy of Forms as the fullest expression of the capacity of thought, thinking will take us to the absolute. Once one starts thinking openly and expansively reality emerges. And it emerges fully formed, for there is no compromise, partiality, incremental progression or false promise involved in reality.

On the face of it this appears to be a paradox. How can thought and reality happily co-exist? Indeed, in most peoples' minds the two are almost mutually exclusive. It is often said that if you think too much you lose touch with reality, the fear of insanity thus becoming a justification for thought-avoidance. It may well be that thought-suppression over the ages was directed in the end, knowingly or not, against the emergence of reality, arguably the most potent threat to any existing order. Thus the Cartesian dictum *cogito ego sum* acquires a new dimension - of thinking through the idea of reality, rather than a mere resolution of doubt or an exercise in epistemology as it is usually taken to be. For Descartes, like any other great philosopher, is a metaphysician at heart, trying to break through to what there is, recognising firstly that it is. Totality being its first feature, reality's inevitability and inescapability is what strikes one, once one turns one's attention to it. This is despite the fact that, built-in across the board, in all senses, in thought, and in the world at large, are defensive structures, filtering mechanisms and screening devices that are meant to dim and modify reality. They seek to make it accessible, render it digestible, delay impact, translate, dress in appearance and create illusions.

Reality and mind collude in creating a semblance, behind which lurks the absolute certainty of execution, of emergence, of full impact. We all know and feel, some say dread, the momentum accrued, the incremental build-up, the steady accumulation, the wave of reality that, once begun, is unstoppable. Thus, we seem to live on the edge of a precipice, realising as we take a step any which way that at the end of the road lies reality itself. The game of avoidance in the face of inevitability is the suspension of life at its very core. Hence the idea of process, of at once opening up all possibilities and at the same time knowing what waits at the end of all manoeuvres, machinations, politics, and flirtations. Thus, the human condition seems to have to involve a suspension of judgement, a state of void, a philosophy of the absurd – precisely because it is evidently clear that there is substance, essence, meaning, response and affirmation *wherever we turn.* And thus the Platonic notion of (re)turn, which means - keep moving (turning), as a sure way of arriving.

II

We relate to reality as if we are trapped with it inside a confined space, something like a large shoe box. The philosophical method is to describe it as though we are looking in from outside. This angle mitigates the human-centred disposition we usually display and allows reality to observe us. Human centred-ness leads to a solipsistic, circular intellectual journey around our present thoughts as conditioned by old psychological wounds. The centre of gravity of reality lies outside us, even while reality includes us; we do well to let the outside configure our world.

Otherwise the convolutions are endless. Not only does mind see reality but it sees reality within mind itself. Consciousness inflates reality, a capacity that comes to the fore in humans, though it is present in the material world according to the Stoics, even in rocks. Consciousness is an aspect of reality that reflects itself; we are intoxicated with our consciousness. As we look at reality we may see more of it and more of consciousness at the same time. Moreover, reality hides or masks itself or reveals itself in fragments. Lacan argues that the emergence of consciousness in the infant marks the end of pure reality as it would otherwise have been. In other words, we pay a price for becoming conscious by losing an ability to remain real.

But we can in fact go beyond merely saying reality is actual and omniscient. Indeed, it is not an anthropomorphic statement but a recognition of the meaning of totality to say reality reaches out to us. Reality watches us; it constantly wants to reveal itself. It seeps into every corner of life, including mind. It is not too much to say that it creates us and ultimately pulls all the strings. At this point the human-centred preoccupation with subjectivity loses its attraction; reality is not our witted creation. There is certainly a sense in which we can and do meet reality somewhere in the middle, where our reaching for it connects with it as it reaches out to us. At this point the epistemological split between subject and object breaks down as the subject becomes part of the object. The idea of subjectivity weakens and collapses; it becomes clear that it has always been a red herring.

The overarching idea presented in the following pages is that reality is all there is: nothing lies outside it: it is infinite. This idea questions the Christian view (echoed in Hegel) that says that when people became aware of themselves they rejected or neglected the paradisiacal, unified world they had once inhabited. Reality, this view insists, split apart; we humans are the cause, consequence and observer of that split.

To say that there is no such split is not to oppose this belief or to make a counter claim; it is a plea to examine reality further. Underlying the idea of a split is a failure to appreciate the complexity of reality. Many elements coexist in reality, some more salient than others at any given moment. Nonetheless, the complexity of reality does not negate the fact that, by definition, it also unites all the elements (for example, consciousness and unconsciousness) because they are merely different aspects of reality itself. An old story illustrates this point. Eight blind Indians were asked to describe what an elephant looked like as each was directed to a different part of the elephant. One said an elephant is like a trunk, another it is like a thin tail, and so on. None could describe the whole animal. But someone able to apprehend the whole could describe it. The task of philosophy is to apprehend reality without let or hindrance such that we realise we are already immersed in it.

This is of course difficult. Firstly, everything is real and nothing more real than anything else. If I think something (that unicorns exist, for instance) there is something there to be thought. Creations of the mind are as real as the mind itself. Secondly, we make unhelpful assumptions about our relation to reality, such as assuming we have to go through disharmony to get to harmony, as does Heidegger. This assumption is associated with the fear that, as we move deeper into ourselves (towards the Freudian id), we will find disturbance, something requiring psychological intervention, in religious terms the source of sin. Yet sin means to miss the mark, not to do wrong. When we perceive disturbance all that has happened is that we have not yet found our place. Suffering (or sin) is what we encounter when we are invested in the world and are thereby split from reality. We are immersed in reality yet are mesmerised by our partial sense of it, which we call the truth. On the other hand, we might subscribe to an idea of diversity or to a postmodern sense of relativism. But diversity is over-determined. Society (even formal philosophy) aims at a level of truth that privileges singularity and thereby creates the very split between truth and untruth that it seeks to repair.

The question of mind recurs. It is dealt with fully in Chapters Five to Seven. This is because it becomes necessary to face the question at the outset of any philosophical foray: is mind a unique phenomenon or a qualitative leap as it were – inserting into the world a dualist polarity? Or conversely is it a 'thing' like any other, inherently unable to alter the nature of the universe as an indivisible whole? If the latter is the case, then the Sphinx-like riddle of 'mind,' like any other puzzle of its kind, can be no more than a ‘shadow on the wall’ in the proverbial Platonic cave.

III

The relation between mind and reality has given rise to a variety of philosophical positions, and may well underpin the nature of philosophy itself. The rise of consciousness and the postmodernist ‘event’ are two examples where the presentation-of-mind has come to replace the more intuitive notion of mind-as-representation in recent discussion.

There is no time sequence or genealogy that posits mind arising out of reality and claiming independent status. The Pre-Socratic Greeks intuited reality as they came to reflect on this big idea. It is as if one day they woke up (or became conscious) and asked themselves: what does it mean to be real? They began to create a set of concepts around the idea of harmony. With that thought they became aware. They allowed something to happen that most cultures turn away from. Arguably they could stand more reality than other people. From that point onwards philosophy was ‘on the table,’ inescapably not fiction nor confined within the bounds of an intellectual discipline. It grew in the gap between reality and everything else. Reality impresses upon us that there is at one and the same time a presence and an immanent nothingness. Philosophy is born out of that gap.

Reality is a supposition, an *a priori*. To attempt to define it as something existing already misses the point because we are then assuming we are outside it and separate from it. It includes all we wish or dream about, because all is in reality. Children open up to the world as wonder; the more they look, the more they see. Reality for them is ever-expanding. Childhood appears as a time when reality exceeds what we are told it is. As we grow older social constraints from without morph into mental ones within, perceptions are subject to categorisation, wholesale scepticism develops, the real diminishes as estrangement follows a constant regress to that which our mind sanctions. There is a tendency to set one's feet on the ground, swap potentiality for actuality, and retreat to a point where nothing lies beyond what can be constructed linguistically. This latter conforms to what Kierkegaard calls the ethical (or middle) stage of life.

However Kierkegaard allows for a third stage of expansive contemplation, a deeper settling into reality as obligations fall away and the social world loses its grip. His ethical stage points to arguably the chief enemy of philosophy – social life. Philosophers see beyond the cave: a life of phenomena is not enough. We can dance, walk in the sun, party, socialise, in other words be preoccupied with feelings or the *presentation* of our bodies; yet all this might only be a romanticising or numbing of the pain of our displacement from reality. When we wait without urgency philosophy listens and remembers, and returns us to living.

Philosophy incorporates all oppositions. It is not concerned to point out that one is right and another wrong, but rather to be indifferent to difference as a fundamental issue. Of course there is a lot of consciousness in reality: after all, hypothesising allows us to philosophise. But in its search for reality philosophy is more interested in the method used than the conclusions reached (which will always be questioned further and eventually incorporated into a greater whole). Philosophers seek to upgrade the question rather than stay attached to an answer, indeed any answer. Concepts are seen as richer, more complex and more yielding of greater depths when they are not immediately translatable into human experience. Reality is inexhaustible and there are infinite ways in which it can be thought about. But human beings conceive everything in nature (including themselves) either as a construct of thought or as a physical object. Yet everything is animated by a scale of complexity ranging from the most simple, such as elementary particles, up to complex physical systems. Equally, thought (including desire and perception) ranges from rudimentary appetites for nourishment or sex (desires) and particular reactions to environment (perception) up to fully articulated desires and beliefs of human beings. Moreover appetites can themselves become conscious and articulate and also become objects of thoughtful reflection.

It deserves repeating that mind is a part of reality. It is unique in that it has developed language and narrative. Thus, philosophy comes into an already-created field of thinking. It removes itself from the fray in order to function. In effect it jumps over consciousness. As philosophy approaches reality this process of engagement returns reality to itself. Claims to possession of an individual mind emerge as the problem. We impose our 'personal mind' on mind in general (so that Kant was half right). However, in contradistinction, Plato situated mind vis a vis reality. My point is that mind is a part of reality. Of course consciousness lies in every aspect of reality that we look at or consider. The dynamics of consciousness dictate that when we look at anything beyond consciousness (Kant only looked at consciousness; Hegel was fascinated by it) the part of reality that is consciousness and the part that is not might appear to be separate. Yet, the story of the eight blind Indians tells us that as we continue to look further we see much more.

A split is a definitional issue. If split means dichotomy then consciousness as part of reality might differ in degree or kind from other parts of reality. But it still remains an aspect of reality. It is in this spirit of unity that philosophy seeks inclusivity of conceptual frameworks. Moore explains that making sense of things includes 'enjoying a kind of indissolubility…the way in which the sheer non-specificity of "things" can put us in mind of simply making sense.' (1) Differences are taken to the level of a meta-concept and ultimately under Spinoza's 'aspect of eternity' where difference becomes insignificant. A cup is a cup and a saucer is a saucer; but both are utensils. A utensil is a utensil and a napkin a napkin but they are both dining accoutrements. And so on, until concepts cancel each other out and we enter reality unfettered, repeating the journey Plato embarked upon.

To say that all is reality is a tautology. It does not make a claim in defence of either side of a dichotomy. It keeps doors open. But, to say that all is consciousness is to confuse categories. Admittedly, it is an approach that arose in the Axial Age (2) at roughly the same time as philosophy; but it lays claim to reality in a singular, anthropocentric way and openly admits that it expresses our individual minds. It is prejudiced by definition and already contains a problem be3cause it leads to practices like the emptying of the mind, without telling us about the relation of mind to reality or what reality is once the mind is emptied. Is there, for example, no substance in the universe? Consciousness doesn't critique itself (a key philosophical practice) and it thus negates the process of conceptual change. The presumption that reality is consciousness puts the cart before the horse, replacing discourse and critique with a narrative approach to reality by presuming we already know what reality is. It cannot accept the idea that reality is not *what* there is (as if there is a choice or an alternative) but *that* there is (it is totality, all that there is). Philosophy says that the journey towards an acceptance that reality is totality is taken in wonder (and never ends), a perpetual uncovering provoked by curiosity. Reality is not limited by existence (people's experiences, biographies, parentage, mind or politics). The message is: 'don't live by smallness.' Reality is liberating, all-inclusive, exciting, and maybe also disturbing, provoking and perplexing. There is something in reality that encourages things to intermingle. Its complexity and capacity for internal refraction mean that things are not necessarily what they appear, are not themselves or at any moment *pronouncedly* real. Even so, at the core of our lives, and given our penetration by mind, we can't go further without facing it. The early Greeks welcomed reality, it is claimed, because they seem to have been more courageous than most human beings. (3) If life has ever seemed a let-down it may be that what is wanted is not more money, exotic experiences, visceral challenges or even silence, but more courage to open to reality.

IV

Can we relate to reality without the intercession of mind? Or, to put the question another way: can we connect to the observed without the need of an observer? This question presupposes we can claim a place outside reality, a kind of Archimedes' Lever, which allows us to look in from the outside. Another question then arises; can we claim to stay within reality but at the same time remain able to think reflexively? Let us go further (philosophy allows this) and wonder if we can in fact face both inwards and outwards at the same time? After all, reality includes both the genius whom society says touches reality and the madman whom society says loses touch with reality. These questions cannot be answered dogmatically, but they can be explored.

Classical philosophy approached the givenness of reality in full recognition of what Socrates called our loss of memory of what it means to partake in it. Philosophy is engrossed in finding a method to address this forgetfulness. Do we for example peel away the layers of socialised debris that cover it? This approach is encapsulated in the famous Greek idea that a sculptor does not impose a form already in his mind onto the marble but scrapes away the material to find a form that already lies there. Or can we add more reality to the small amount we have allowed to enter our lives? Plato describes people leaving a cave where reality was so wan it amounted to the flickering of shadows on the wall. The cave-dwellers moved out into the sunlight. However we construe the issue it is to mind we seem first to turn to as we engage beyond the self. And yet mind is an unreliable instrument. Could it be that when we talk of leaving Plato's Cave and entering the sunlight we are actually referring to putting the mind back into the body? This is the focus of the next chapter.

CHAPTER THREE - THE BODY

For 2500 years the mind has reigned supreme as the centre-piece of philosophy. At the outset of that period it seemingly 'broke away' from the body and formed consciousness, as expressed in the work of Anaxagoras, Plato, Aristotle and Descartes. Yet, even the originator of the Cogito was never committed to a total breach. Admitting that the mind is easier to know than the body, Descartes added nonetheless: '…I am not only lodged in my body, like a pilot in his ship, but, besides, that I am joined to it very closely and indeed so compounded and intermingled with my body, that I form, as it were, a single whole with it.' Everything comes down to the relation of mind and body. Postmodernity wants to right the balance: it now tells us that the conceptualisation of mind has gone too far. So, where neuroscience raises mind to the level of meta-cognition, philosophy instead returns to the point before mind rose to such splendid pre-eminence. It seeks to locate thinking before mind waylaid it. At that distant point thought was only one of many capacities in the body. The anchoring of thought in the body has come down to us along three intellectual route-ways.(1) One is animalism; another materialism/physicalism; a third is a post-Spinoza commitment to a body that thinks.

Eagleton sees an animalist thread running through philosophy from Aquinas to Marx, Nietzsche and Wittgenstein. John Gray can be added to this list. The physicalist/materialist route is presently being taken by Antonio Damasio and Eagleton himself. (2) Both these routes however treat the body as sensate but not animate. Materialism is a dualist concept, being the opposite of mind. Both approaches fail to understand Spinoza's quest (the third route) to see the body as animated.

I

I want to bring the thinking body to the forefront of philosophical discourse without recourse to dualist or physical notions such as the neurology of the brain. Of course, the question has always arisen at some point: how can we philosophise without observing physiological aspects of the body? One provocation to write this book was Spinoza's question: what can the body do? My proposition is that the primordial wholeness sensed by the Greeks manifests in the body that channels thought. Spinoza's monism cannot be ignored; there can be no going back to the mind-body division introduced in the Axial Age. Critiques of monism must now incorporate the idea of 'bodying forth' of Heidegger, emergent properties that arise in assemblages as described by Deleuze or the unity of the lived body as described by Merleau-Ponty. For a century and a half a suggestion has hung in the air but never finally been asserted that the body's ability to channel reflective forces is merely one among many other of its connections to the world that include the hormonal, immune, nervous and endocrine systems.

The body is nature, a visceral, vital, animated and complex nexus of energy. By being anchored within nature it is more powerfully immune to artifice than is mind. (3) Spinoza's rejection of the Cartesian Cogito gave philosophy a glimpse of what body-centred-ness can mean. He was aware that the mind is drawn to a sense of oneness with the universe and that the mind, in religious parlance, sees the body as fallen or exiled. Mind, Spinoza seems to be saying, wants to know body, in that it is aware that it itself is not body. Nonetheless, as Spinoza's thinking indicates, it recognises that the body's rootedness makes it superior to mind. The mind is able to view things from this angle only because it is severed or dissociated from nature.

However, when the mind observes the body, the mind becomes aware of itself as an observer; this creates a gap which mind seeks to close. This is a source of confusion about the body. Intermingling of functions can still leave mind as a separate part or category of the body. Antonio Damasio has argued for the possibility that the body has a greater part to play in the organism relative to the mind. But he stops before placing the mind in the body. Deleuze and Guattari's ideas of affective connections, planes of immanence and organisation, virtual-actual and bodies-without-organs complements Merleau-Ponty's reference to the 'I' being an intersubjective field only because of the body. Together they place the body in the world. Again, Deleuze and Merleau-Ponty's use of planes of signification to indicate the relation of mind to body, rather than categories, orders or sorts of reality, deepens the relationship between thought and body. Moreover, by claiming that the body contains pre-reflective powers Merleau-Ponty opened up further fruitful possibilities. Yet, in the end both thinkers are dualists. Thought and body may overlap or entwine and not be categorically separate and might even possess pre-reflective powers, but there is no sense here of a body that thinks. Most tellingly, both thinkers believed body and thought were ultimately united only in art. (4)

What for example are the implications for the body of the mind loosening its grip on thinking? I take it that this is where Spinoza's question about what a body can do takes us. Yet even he fudged the issue by making body and thought aspects of the same thing, God. Dual-aspect monism has been dogged with controversy ever since and still enjoys a very mixed press. One can understand why: there has to be something real, a 'that it is' rather than a 'what it is,' a unity that embraces all mind-schisms. The world cannot only be viewed through the lens of ideology, materialism or psychology, for they are all mind-constructs themselves. Only at the point of 'that it is' can philosophy ask the big questions.

II

Indeed, some things can already be said – the body has evolved; there is no mystery about that. We can also accept that the mind is an idea that has developed to accommodate thinking as a detached function a la Descartes. Moreover, given that most thinking, even that which lies beneath the thin veneer of personal opinion and idiosyncrasy, comprises socially-defined, repetitive and conformist mantras, we can reverse the usual saying and suggest that minds have been taken over by society while bodies are individual. Psychosomatically, bodies carry deep messages concerning that which has been unprocessed by thinking. Additionally, we have moved beyond talking about mind-body splits a la Descartes. We can also let go of the notion that mind is the God-like aspect of humans and body is something we drag along behind us. Body has evolved attributes and modes, many layers of functionality, as an outcome of evolution. So, some movement is possible: an emergent monism along the lines of Spinoza can be seen as not a huge intellectual leap. What then is stopping us going further to where, we might postulate, Spinoza himself wanted to go? This would involve integrating the division between body and thought into a unity that is now only body. Body is no longer a machine with ratios or intermeshing of different parts, but a lived life. When I say 'I am conscious' I am not speaking from some free-floating cognitive base but from within the body itself. Body is now the subject, not the object of thought. In this case, the long-sustained idea of a detached mind can at last be dispensed with. Indeed, it can be placed in the arena of what will in Section Three be described as the socio. The very idea of mind is dualist, that is, it is separate from the body. In other words, the idea derives from a splitting of the body's functions. When the world is viewed through the prism of mind the world appears to be riven by innumerable dichotomies.

Attempts during the last 100 years to go beyond Spinoza's position have been held back by the dualist thinking that runs through the philosophical and scientific canons. The ideas of materialism and panpsychism stand at opposite extremes on a wide spectrum that makes it impossible to move towards unity. Heidegger's attempt to unite Being as both a universal idea and a human life left a gap between the two. He was forced to evolve an indeterminate and romantic context in which both could co-exist. Wittgenstein wanted to anchor thought in the body, (5) in appreciation of the profound implications of the phrase 'that it is,' without being able to proffer a context in which this arose in the lived life. Damasio has recently offered support to a re-interpretation of Spinoza's monism that is tilted towards the body. However he seeks to find ways to accommodate both the underlying physicalism of neuroscience (associated with the brain) and the reflexive capacity I describe as mind, when both (including the mind) are themselves mind-constructs. He settles on feelings as the way bodies express their grounded-ness and thus, by focusing on one expression of the body (and one susceptible to socially-conformist thinking) avoids a thorough-going move to the body. (6) The dualism at the heart of neuroscience, German Idealism and analytic philosophy and a persistent holding onto subjectivity across much of current philosophy prevents the body from being seen as the conduit of thought. Followers of Freud extended to the world at large the structures he believed were located in consciousness. This idea has been applied to the body in much of current thought. The body's functions have to be seen to be split or segregated to permit this idea to hold. But, as has been explained in earlier chapters, splits are not built *into* the mind (and therefore by extension are not built into the universe). They are *products of the mind*, that is to say, products of thinking that has itself succumbed to order and structure. Belief that the mind and the world are pre-emptively split preserves the ascendency of mind in philosophy and in society. The argument presented in subsequent pages however is that, only when the body is seen as an organism containing a stabilising network of integrated functions operating both internally and in connection with the world, all of which permits it to act as a transmitter of universal thought, can the 'I' engage fully with reality.

CHAPTER FOUR - PHILOSOPHY AND HUMAN WELLBEING

Why be concerned about reality during the course of our daily lives? Because, I suggest, we realise that human agency arises only when we accept that the world reaches out to us and not the other way round. When we realise the world is not a human-centric creation we enhance our wellbeing. We can only do this by taking reality as a given and by refraining from treating it as a thing. Plato did not invent or discover reality; he discovered the mind that conceives of reality as an idea. But reality is all there is; it is the milieu we move within. The ultimate One who conceives of things might be claimed as God. If life is about suffering then it might be argued that God the parent is flawed and we humans are a mistake. But *we are here.* This is not in doubt. Philosophy is not concerned with a creator but with what is created, creation itself. When we take reality as given we can then look at what Man has made of it and, by stripping away all that he has accumulated, find what the world truly is. Therein lies wonder. This may be a task without limit. And yet we have turned away from it towards the working of mind without understanding the deleterious effect this move has on human wellbeing. When we turn away from recognising that reality is a given, that it is everything there is, when instead we start to think about it, we become fascinated by the mind. And in so doing we become fascinated by ourselves, the observers, and very soon we mistake solipsism for reality. And then we become distressed. An example of thinking that takes reality as a given and only then sought our place in the universe was found in early Greece. They claimed we are free when we find our true place in the universe, a place that awaits us. It already exists, but not as a defined place, ascertainable by computation or located with regard to other things. It is not even to be found by intellectual brilliance, ardent willpower or happenstance. In other words, searching for answers or leaving things to chance will not take us there. But, letting as much reality in as we can bear, and then learning to stretch and embrace even more, can however do this.

I

Searching for answers - a propensity which is very strong in philosophy and takes the form of creating and adding to a canon of knowledge - has weakened its capacity to enhance human wellbeing. In fact, the search for knowledge has turned philosophy into just one university discipline among others. In this sense the first fatal step was Plato's creation of his Academy. Yet, philosophy is only marginally concerned to accumulate or verify knowledge. The latter is a tool that reminds human beings of their place within the wholeness of things. It is not a discipline in the sense that other university subjects are - breaking off sections of knowledge and creating a discipline-specific method and language to go with it - but it rides above them, recognising their methods and raisons d'etre as but fragments of philosophical wholeness. Without philosophy's capacity to embrace and contextualise its component parts, the hubris of these binary fragments will engender the split minds that cause distress. Only by allowing thinking to embrace wholeness can philosophy offer more than temporary, physical or cosmetic relief to distress. Everything else on offer is a chimera: capitalism offers us love when we buy goods we mostly do not need; culture lauds a sentimentalising selfhood; scientism and academe abide by nullifying peer-review.

However, questioning our suppositions has the power to clear a way through uncritical thinking that gives us the impression we are the centre of the universe. Philosophy is not subjective or human-centred. It is true that all its questions are carved out of the lived life. But it sees reality as expressed in the subject rather than projected by the mind onto an object outside. And, crucially, this is a subject defined by its receptivity of all that lies outside. In other words, reality lies in a body that thinks, as (very nearly) Spinoza expressed it. Only when we are an open, receiving subject can reality enter. We might grow up trying to push aside our parents, siblings, colleagues or friends in order to build an identity and ego but we can't 'kill-off' everyone around us in order to feel safe or powerful. A degree of otherness always remains unconquerable. Mother was there when the baby was born; in other words, self is already relational. It follows that, as I think deeper into myself, I find another there; as I look even deeper I encounter radical alterity. We can challenge the perceiving eye by putting another person before our self and starting to ask about other people's problems, rather than by striving to authenticate our own sense of self. Once we authenticate the other we might notice we are also authenticating the other in ourselves. We can then, like Socrates, invite others to critique us in order further to break down the edifice of self and to open to reality. When we let otherness assume a place in our lives we are, it can be said, letting reality enter us.

In this sense, philosophy is the unfolding of the difficulty of being alive. Philosophy doesn't know what philosophy is: it is not an object. It thus needs an anchor; this lies in the fulcrum method of metaphysics which is explained in Chapters Twelve and Thirteen. This method eschews asking what reality is and looks instead at what humankind has thought about it; and only then asks the biggest questions about these ideas. Philosophy is more practical in the long run than for instance administrative solutions because it makes sure we do not make unsubstantiated claims.

II

Thinking did not arise with the appearance of humans. One does not need to claim that consciousness is everything in order to appreciate that rocks and lakes can think and that human beings partake of consciousness rather than generate it personally. As such, human freedom manifests when we know without question that we are part of the whole, a whole that preceded 'my' thinking. Freedom manifests in those moments when I say, 'Ah, yes, that is just so, it couldn't be otherwise!' A certainty obtains that has nothing to do with strength of assertiveness, adept use of rules of argumentation, or quickness of responding to lacunae in a discussion. These moments of clarity or certainty may be rare but the possibility surely exists to extend them throughout one's day. In such moments calmness and immediacy combine to leave one fascinated rather than overwhelmed by what others might see as extreme duress. Thus, it would follow that harmony is the way that philosophising manifests in life. It amounts to engaging fully with whatever is happening without panicking. In these moments, just as in less tense moments, one's thinking continues to process what is happening. I mean that those moments are ever-there, waiting to be experienced when one is congruent with all that is happening. One does not create or engineer them – that would be an act of will in which one mistakenly puts a claim to a personal mind at the centre of things. The obstacles that stop one being immediate to reality lie in one's thinking. As reason in the sense Kant uses it is perhaps over-strict it might have been better, in terms of the ideas I want to develop henceforth, to use the word thinking. Looking back on these moments of congruency, people often use phrases like 'Yes, things have their time.' But is congruence a matter of timing? Certainly, these moments can't be forced or grasped at; we seem always to overreach an objective where the ego is concerned. They can be brought under the heading of synchronicity when viewed with the benefit of hindsight; body and thought come together to allow for, say, the exercise of (hitherto hidden) natural authority or for one to say or do just what one wants to say or do without contradiction or doubt, and without, ironically, being over-aware of thinking. What is said nestles within the harmony of a group or a relationship without being subjected to an overweening superego or self-consciousness. Franz Rosenzweig describes it as: 'Still totally opened, still empty, still without content, without essence, pure readiness, pure obedience, all ear.' (1) Yet, harmony does not appear to have a philosophical basis (although of course it has a central place in mythos), until we acknowledge that a sense of unity, of being at one with the world, arises just in these moments.

Philosophy traditionally provided for human wellbeing by reducing the anxiety generated by an over-excited mind. Revealingly, the most obvious connection between philosophy and the lived life arises when the threat of personal disintegration is most intense. This connection is manifested in the very moment of encounter between two strangers. That moment is commonly experienced as a panic wherein we feel compelled to make an impromptu judgement about the other. On the basis of this rushed decision we 'place' the other as likable or otherwise and our relationship becomes ossified. Thus we close down the possibility of wonder. This is the philosophical moment where bifurcation or duality might appear and we enter the realm of the socio, a realm that is immensely difficult to vacate once entered. In modern times, at the micro-level, the ramifications of this event usually become the justification for psychological intervention. Yet Socrates was at the greatest of pains to show that this was where philosophy came into its own. He did this by constantly setting dogmatic ideas, ego and subjectivity into the context of the universe. That is to say, by showing that reality is the big picture, the anchor to which all thinking is secured, and that to put one's self at the centre of the universe is to bifurcate life and the universe, to feel isolated and thereby to invite distress. Theorising emerges from intense and agitated thinking, according to my thesis; Spinoza explains it as no longer being at one with the universe. Spinoza and Rosenzweig equate over-excited thinking with loneliness. Indeed, my claim that adequate thinking and immediacy of living are inter-related recurs in various guises within the canon of philosophy. Nietzsche reveals it in his distrust of philosophy professors and of abstract concepts like being; Heidegger is saying this when he endeavoured to bring being into everyday life; and it is there in Wittgenstein's call for philosophy to become an activity. Theorising was Plato's way of intellectualising Socrates' encounters in the *Agora* and the homes of his friends. Theorising manifests in the fascination with dualism and its child, subjectivity, a concept that has dominated the canon for 350 years. Yes, there is a growth in philosophy as an aid-to-living or consolation, but the view that life is nothing if it not philosophical, as the Greeks told us, is today encountered only in the margins of official philosophy and it needs discovering all over again. The next three chapters will pick up this theme by asking why we see mind as our connection to reality when its distortions are apparent every day in divisiveness and acrimony.

SECTION TWO: MIND

CHAPTER FIVE - MIND AND PHILOSOPHY

When approached with a cultivated mind philosophy begins in wonder and wholeness. Thinking that is free of the constraints an uncultivated mind imposes enables one to live in magnificence. However, philosophy's failure to prevent an insistent drift towards academicism, as mentioned in the Introduction, is but the tip of an iceberg. More seriously, below the water-line, philosophy has become fascinated by what mind tells us. The result is that, as was discussed in Chapter One, philosophy has lost its anchor in reality. This is the more difficult to address because it is barely acknowledged. A harmonious life can be defined as one in which connection to other human beings is clean and sharp; where the human search for connection and the metaphysical search for the true nature of things are one and the same thing. They both express the way that totality manifests itself. Everything else – particularity, selfhood, and especially mind, are merely *parts* or *fragments* of the whole, manifestations of reality without separate ontological status. Because totality is inclusive it is able to embrace all the particularities created by the dualist tendency of an uncritical mind. All the same, particularities and dualisms cannot be other than parts of the whole. It is at this point that it becomes imperative to address the relation between mind and philosophy. It is not uncommon to hear it said that mind is the originator of thinking. My point is that unfettered thinking precedes mind.

I

What then is unfettered thinking? It is energy thrusting itself into the world. It is drive, Olympian superabundance, Dionysian overflow, and the energy released in the moment of Heidegger's 'unconcealment.' It is what is revealed or released in the space that Socrates' interrogation opened up in the mind of his interlocutor; it arose when Socrates said that he knew that he knew nothing. It is what arises when thinking is thrown beyond constraints of the mind by the fulcrum move. (1) This kind of thinking is distinctive. It does not aim to produce anything, such as opinions, ideas, positions or doctrines; it owes no allegiance to its originator; it connects with its opposite; it stands empathetically and not competitively between parts; it connects with where things come from.

Where does thinking start? True or fresh thinking manifests from nothing. (2) At the point where Socrates' interrogations broke down the defences of his interlocutor and a stunned silence followed - the process known as *aporia* - the mind retreated and allowed new, perhaps uniquely new, thinking to appear. Following the moment of *aporia,* and maybe *in* that moment, the possibility of a fresh start, a new hypothesis, arises. By its nature a hypothesis cannot arise wholly out of prior knowledge. Indeed, a hypothesis may be described as a moment when reason meets flux, when organised thinking meets undefined flow. To the degree that it is not knowledge-based it falls into the area of nothing.

Already implicit in the new hypothesis, in the fresh start, is the structured, ordered thinking that I call mind. An upsurge in fresh thinking seems always to trigger a counter-reaction. This reaction generates logic, meaning and ethics; the reaction quickly forgets that it originally arose from fresh thinking and it starts to shackle the latter by imposing structures on it. In no time at all thinking has become mind – thinking that imposes rules in order to achieve definition. The counter-reaction has become a complex structured product comprising many layers. An analogy might serve: if we go back to the age of myths we can begin to see how both thinking and philosophy arose. Villagers, after becoming a little tired of listening to individual stories of itinerant storytellers, were drawn at some point to a deeper story that they sensed lay beneath all the individual ones. I'll call this underlying story - logos. At first this deeper story/logos confused the listeners because it forced them to address general issues of storytelling, such as text, idea, meaning and thinking systems. Here is philosophical thinking emerging – to do with the whole – but also mind emerging as a defence against philosophical thinking – to do with the analytic of story-writing and -telling. Equally, logos embraces particularities and fractures, but it also brings dualisms derived from logic into philosophical thinking. In other words, thinking's original, primordial energy takes us into virgin territory whilst at the very same time taking us backwards, in this case to the age of myths. The action of mind has recently provoked such a backwards-and-forwards-at-the-same-time movement in philosophy – postmodernism – which is fascinated by language and narrative, which are treated at one and the same time as restricting and yet opening up philosophical thought. This backward reach of mind has also taken us forwards in time to neuroscience's attempt to locate mind in one organ of the body on the one hand and to recent mind-fascinated schools of philosophy such as transcendental-materialism on the other.

Whether or not theories of mind are accurate is not at issue here. Much more serious is the effect that mind has of dragging philosophy into becoming a theory of mind. Theory of mind is only a small branch of philosophy. Mind is indeed a big concept, but it is only one among many others, such as truth, courage and justice. My point is that philosophy is greater than any of its branches and is independent of mind. Heidegger points in this direction, telling us that mind may be a poor guide to reality and that, if we relax and do not search for anything, all will be revealed. He moreover describes reality as active and as reaching out to us. The most that mind can then be is an imperious doorkeeper.

II

Wonder might be said to arise in the beholding, without reserve, of everything in totality. Thus philosophy arises in the moment I open my eyes and apprehend the world around me *before* my reflexive thinking starts to tell me that I am not part of what I apprehend. I apprehend something that preceded my apprehension: thinking opens to reality. If I begin to think of what I apprehend as beyond the mind – alterity - I am responding to the call of reality. I do not need to challenge the a *priori a* nature of infinity (it precedes my thoughts) because my thinking is capable of expanding thoughts into meta-ones, potentially all the way to infinity. Though my thinking travels in this direction – from immediate to infinite - the infinite has always been there waiting for me to think it. Yet, what am I thinking? Thought is not a product of my mind because mind is an instrument of thought. My thoughts do not originate from within my mind; my mind responds to what enters it via thought. To be in awe thus arises as my thinking connects with what my senses let in of the world that has escaped the constraints of mind.

When this matter is approached slightly differently we can say we are dealing with intra-subjectivity. A close relationship breaks down my perceptions of a barrier between myself and others and creates room for awe to arise. This is the territory of Levinas' 'Other' which channels the call of reality. Awe is my response to the call of reality, to what a religious believer would call God. In this intra-personal space of wonder I am invited to love more of what is non-me or outside of me. Moreover, in this space I realise that, just as I think and feel, so does everyone else think and feel too; I am a manifestation of reality, but so are others too. The more I open to this alterity the more I overcome narcissism. And to the extent that I let go of my narcissism I become a reflective, rational being. My relation to the Other has opened me to the infinite and the eternal in the way that in earlier times was explained by reference to soul.

Now it becomes difficult to see myself as a discrete subject, and certainly not a self, as if I stand entirely outside the reality I apprehend. I am part of the reality that I perceived initially 'outside' me. To hold to a sense of subjectivity would be to mistake myself as agent, initiator or bestower of meaning. Indeed, if I claim to be separate from the universe I must now represent totality in a fractured or binary way. So, as I begin thinking, my thoughts expand until they are concepts and the concepts serve as a muse that connects me to the world. They open up discourse. Of course this discourse includes giving attention to dichotomising concepts like a gap between subject and object that might still survive in me as a trace of subjectivity that society has persuaded me to hold onto. Yet, even so, I am free to stop short of legitimising or reifying these traces even as I notice them. The universe is all; thinking is a capacity within it. Of course, if thinking were to expand so that it *corresponded* to reality (where Plato seems to have been taking us) then we could use the terms thinking and reality interchangeably. We would be free of mind. Therein we can relax and, as Heidegger advises, let reality reach out to us in a two-way connection that is immanent with potential.

III

This book asks what it means to live in reality. There needs to be a point or core of being to relate from and to. Until we open to it we will be at the mercy of mind-distractions and of the socio (of which more later). To illustrate this point I will compare two statements. Statement One: I awake in the morning to a world *which* is. The word 'which' in this statement is a questioning one; it privileges my subjective stance and makes the universe into an object of my gaze. We can now ask if the world is truly there and if we can agree on its meaning. This position assumes I can think myself into a position that stands outside the universe. This is the dualist stance. Statement Two: I awake in the morning to a world *that* is. This statement acknowledges the world as a given or presupposition, an already or *a priori*, that embraces any attempt I might make to claim to stand outside it. I respond to reality that just is; I am unable to contextualise, analyse or split it.

Dualisms put mind at the centre of things. Heidegger rejected the metaphysics that dominated western thought from Descartes down to the 1960s because it places mind as subject and reality as object. Monism posits things the other way around: reality is the subject and mind is merely the object; mind is a part that obstructs or calibrates a re-entry into connected-up reality. Thus, the universe observes us rather than the other way round. But to say this boldly misses out the inter-relations and complexities that it will be the purpose of this book to unfold.

Yes, the mind can be a fickle, unresponsive instrument, seemingly unsuited as a tool to clear away what keeps us from the givenness of reality. But this is no reason to forsake the cultivating of mind with this purpose in view. Cultivation of mind can lay claim to be the prime function of philosophy. Until life is grounded in reality it gets stuck between the Scylla of remote, precise, textual minutiae to which official philosophy (and institutional life and bureaucracy) is prone, and the Charybdis of overblown and unexplained emotions to which the crowd is prone. The latter will be treated later in the chapters dealing with the socio. Philosophy has always been about the way we use our minds to understand the relation between mind and reality. Inescapably, the starting point is an acknowledgement that reality is an *a priori* or a given in our lives. By raising the idea of alterity postmodern thinkers have questioned the meaning of subjectivity. The originating impulse shifted from the subject; but it didn't settle on the object, which is a figment of the dichotomising mind. Instead the Other is now posited as constituting the subject. The Other is a channel through which reality manifests itself in the world. Subjectivity has now lost much of its sense of agency, though postmodernists have generally modified it without being prepared to let go of it altogether. We can now ask: whence does the impulse of life arise, and how does it manifest?

Postmodernism has helped us reconnoitre new ground. And here is where philosophy shows its capacity to reveal what lies beyond, contra Kant, by practising a reversal. Despite the prominence of subjectivity in the philosophical canon, a strand of thinking has persisted from Spinoza to Levinas that reminds us that, far from the human subject being the centre of the universe, he or she is but a manifestation of an a *priori* universe. Features of life such as self, identity and personality are merely attempts to hold on to thinking that has become a prisoner of mind. (3) So, dare we let go of these unhelpful protections and just be? The first move is obviously to ask how reality manifests through us. As indicated above, Levinas suggests that, rather than reality being an abstraction, it manifests itself through the 'Other.' He argues that the Other is someone who is not contained in personal experience, even though 'the common world' never exists in isolation from the Other. (4)

So, returning to the moment I open my eyes – If I perceive the 'beyond me' as reality, conceiving the universe from the vantage of a subject or self, then I will sustain the illusion that these constructs have some kind of independent status vis a vis the universe. My point is that the universe is totality and *a priori*; the universe thinks through a subject. The anchor for everything is always the universe, not any construction of the mind. The lure of mind has been so strong that its propensity to dichotomise wholeness has never irrefutably been seen for what it is - a part claiming to represent the whole. When it is seen in this way, this dichotomising move can be included within the embrace of the universe.

Reality is all around us. And yet in our lived lives we seem condemned in perpetuity to live through cyclical 'discoveries' of it, requiring bouts of tears and distress to snap us out of our reveries. Yet, so many questions are raised by our disengagement from it. For example, do we really need recurrent war to appreciate peace? Is death necessary for an awakening to life? Is the saliency of wrong a pre-condition for the recognition of right? And so on. Powerful but false harbingers of the real lure us away from reality itself; we end up by making pacts with the devil. Thus when we replace being with anything else we betray life. How do we betray? A list would include: bowing before authority; deifying desires; believing perceptions; being self-centred; collapsing into non-relating; codifying logic; being uncurious; giving up; not seeking to understand; sentimentalising the past; being conceptually rigid; succumbing to surges of emotion; losing sight of the whole; pursuing outcomes; arguing; being closed-minded.

CHAPTER SIX - THE DEATH OF GOD AND THE RISE OF MIND

God (or reality) died at or soon after the moment of Creation or the Big Bang: this is Nietzsche's point. It is also possible to claim that the death of God can be read as the birth of mind because the world was not created, so to speak, until a mind could conceive it. Yet, just as he had fully discovered the mind that conceived reality Plato immediately sold the pass by splitting reality into two: concepts and copies (qua epistemology). Nietzsche understood Plato's move however when he realised that, once mind appeared, it persuaded us that it was reality itself, instead of being merely a channel to reality. Before Creation, in the Garden of Eden or Paradise, all was goodness. In this state of bliss there were no splits or polarities; all was flow and harmony. Out of this state the Devil, Evil or mind appeared. Here therefore mind is a representation, not of bad as such, but of our inability to handle excesses of goodness. As explained in the previous chapter it is a counter-move to the thrusting drive of thinking, a kind of safety device that rebounds on its user. The internal flow and turbulent excess of God or Good disturbs the regular disposition that gazes upon it, similar to the way the behaviour of a boisterous child might frighten a well-behaved parent. In overreaction the parent demarcates the child's behaviour into right and wrong. At that moment cosmic mind was born. Nietzsche defined the excess energy as Dionysian, Freud as the id, both forces being easily perceived as frighteningly over-the-top and potentially disruptive of Good. At this point moreover, the philosophical category of epistemology and the artistic concept of mimesis or copy appeared. Both of these forms of thinking subscribe to a belief that reality is accessed by the senses. Both turn reality into a matter of subjectivity, as if it is outside us and yet at the same time personal to us. Put in more down-to-earth terms – it is because we have lost our sense of connection that we fear we will never connect and love properly again. We seek to be totally open to others but we are frightened and only offer them our 'self,' by definition a wanting entity that can only grasp at others. This is coincidentally the moment of birth of culture: rather than connect, we write about connection or compose or paint it. We live as simulacra in a world of mind-determined copies.

Attempts to rectify this situation are rare because, a double irony, we are so preoccupied with the workings of our mind. So, it behoves us before we go any further to ask why we let the content of our mind enter into a discussion of reality. Compared to the ubiquity of reality the content of mind is a small matter. Reality has many properties: it encompasses language, consciousness, mind and thinking. Subjectivity tries to offer the mind's view in place of reality. Mind is real of course; it is part of reality, but only a part. There is nothing else but reality.

Consciousness appeared at the same time as reality - at the big bang. Yet what was also revealed then was that consciousness possesses interrelated elements that are held in suspension by reality itself. However, when consciousness became aware of itself it became frightened. It panicked and created a tainted, autonomous system. This is the substitute for reality that we call the mind. Consciousness attempted to persuade us to accept mind. We should not therefore bother trying to overcome problems of mind; mind is an unnecessary concept; moreover, it is a mutant, a freak. All our 'problems,' such as desire, are products of mind. For example, desire arises as we respond to the other. It is not a natural response; rather it is manufactured in an attempt to calibrate our response to the other.

Problems seem to have arisen at the Big Bang itself. As something dawned, consciousness and cosmos arose simultaneously or very nearly so. An idea of fixity was applied to Creation, as if energy was stolen from somewhere else, and guilt began to accumulate. The emergence of something new had to be seen to pay a price. This is expressed as the death of God. Desire is new growth and, so Freud tells us, we must construct a superego to keep it in its place. In the same vein Aristotle contended that A cannot be both A and B at the same time. Why not? Children know it can. Why do we need to see emergence as a burden, as coming at a price? The story of Pandora's Box carries the same message. Open the box, let new energy emerge, and all hell breaks loose. Why, as Camus asked, is the only choice between going forward or committing suicide? Reality joins us one to another: invade me if you want, you are part of me; and vice versa.

We can say that the mind is divided into its core and the layers surrounding it. However, these layers are not necessarily an extension of the core. Rather they may act in discordance with it. Equally, reality may not manifest itself fully in accordance with its source or nucleus. This is far from mysticism, and in actuality is a close approximation to our understanding of what Wittgenstein refers to as *the state of affairs*. It is important to unravel heterogeneity in things great and small as we enter relational fields, like the fundamental encounter between reality and mind. For, if each contains kernels of the other in itself, our understanding will shift from the notion of struggle, warfare or even encounter, to the more feasible idea of recognition. Indeed, what happens when we see each other in the mirror? Do we believe it to be a reflection, ontologically reduced, or do we grant it reality of sorts, thus allowing it to enhance our knowledge of ourselves and in the process to learn something about the not-me, even if or as it corresponds in all details with our previously-held, pre-mirror-revelation or pre-mirror-notion of ourselves?

I

The modern mind has lost a sense of the real and the not-me - and indeed of itself - to such an extent that the very notion of reality, alterity or otherness seems to have collapsed altogether into what is now termed and glorified as the signifier, which has come to replace that *which it came to signify* in the first place. Thus signification - representation, in old parlance - has turned things around, and our grasp of the simulacrum is seen as the thing-in-itself. To the many who are steeped in humanism and postmodernism there is only mind, which constructs all and sundry 'out there.' We do not and cannot know anything because the mind forever stands in the way, and there is nothing that is not mind-dependent. This thinking tells us that we must only know *ourselves* – everything becomes psychology. It leads to a belief that subjectivity cannot be overcome.

We can however try reversing the process by putting reality at the start of thinking and working our way towards a perceiving-responding and indeed a constructing-creating mind. Reality enjoys the ultimate ontological status. (1) It simply is there. It has always been the task of philosophy to address it. It is eternal, timeless, preceding and outliving, indeed encompassing and incorporating what may well be an all-perceiving, perhaps even an all-knowing, mind. Maybe singular in scope, indeed prototypical of reality itself, mind can nonetheless be overcome with a little humility and self-discipline. As much as we are all full of, indeed fascinated by, ourselves and our power to fantasise and create myths, stories and narratives, there is something significant that outsmarts us in our observer-illusion and places us under its all-embracing gaze. What then can mind know?

We have still to free ourselves of mind. Philosophy retains a methodological leverage to do this. This is because it is more than a catalogue of ideas. It goes deeper: it is a commitment to try and get to reality. Schopenhauer mentions the Veil of Maya that we must sweep aside before we can be real. All thinkers have contributed ideas and built on earlier ones: Plato clarifies the concept of mind; Aristotle offers a classificatory system of knowledge; Aquinas clarifies God, and so on. But still reality is obscured. We are now beginning to see, murkily to be sure, a cause that might make others, such as mind, seem small. This is the socio, the focus of Chapters Eight and Nine.

We know enough about the operation of mind to be able to stop treating it as a project. Mind is only an idea we use when we seek to allocate responsibility to an individual. Comments like 'The I observes reality' or 'Something lies between mind and reality' miss the point; other minds are present each time we believe we are thinking individually. Plurality and the collective mind operate behind the scenes. The concept of an individual collapses when it is implemented in the actuality of the lived life.

CHAPTER SEVEN - THE OPERATION OF MIND

The way that mind operates creates a sense that life is split and that harmony is unattainable. Three examples are offered here to show how the power of the mind leads us away from harmony and towards palliatives such as the appeal of happiness, the intrusion of values into ethics and of knowledge into society.

HAPPINESS

Why bother with reality when by common accord we seek happiness? Levels of unhappiness are said to be unacceptably high. Happiness seems to promise something positive while reality (so far as it is considered at all) is associated with pain or at best a dubious gain. Roger Scruton has written about the capacity of alcohol to soften the harsh outline of reality. Is reality harsh, or does this question miss the point? Let us start with some assumptions. Humanity emerged from the swamp or savannah and formed into packs; thus at the outset there existed multiplicity within the oneness of the universe. A problem thus arises when humanity focuses only on its internal multiplicity. The separate parts cannot bear to look on each other, as Scruton observes. But this is to sink into despair. Is not a conversation between the internal parts, and between inside and outside, only a matter of being committed to go where the conversation takes us? Of course, this requires courage and perseverance. But isn't that a price worth paying for reality?

A doctrine such as happiness is only a premature ending along a spectrum which has reality at its furthest reaches. So why not carry on all the way to reality? Reality is the only venture able to address all our conundrums. Rather than answers we can seek more intimate understanding of the questions. Answers lead only to solutions that beg further questions in infinite regress. Yet the question already contains the origin of what we seek. The riddle of the Sphinx tells us in effect that the ultimate answer to all questions is: 'what you ask is what you are.' We *are* reality.

Reality does not negate happiness but says that happiness offers too narrow a remit by which to live a life. Let go of culture and forced empathy, philosophy says; ignore the gaze of the other that demands we feel guilty. Go further; the gods are calling us to look at life from an Olympian eminence. Accept every gift that life offers – people who cross your path, a new perspective, an insight. If everything within us is real – our imagination or our pain for instance – and we understand the correspondence between such seemingly 'separate' phenomena and other aspects of the whole, both between and within us, then we have achieved the Holy Grail of congruence. The Greek sense of harmony embraces this idea. Logos is thus the equivalent of the harmony that Mythos describes in stories. The capacity of a hypothesis to anchor harmony is equal to that of a mythical story or narrative. We lose touch with reality if we divide, compartmentalise or categorise entities as if they are discrete. So we need an idea or hypothesis that says: in order to become a thing-in-itself we must first have acknowledged our connectedness to other things.

To become real is to appreciate that happiness is an illusion. Only then can we realise that reality offers the only grounds for understanding humanity. In contrast, happiness is temporary, reflecting moods rather than anything intrinsic. It is dependent on the possession of something seen initially as a lack. It can only be contemplated as the price paid for repressing its opposite- unhappiness – the two together comprising the whole. Epistemologically it doesn't make sense to believe in happiness when unhappiness can be perceived all around. Indeed such split thinking is itself the source of untold misery. In effect this idea is saying - if you claim to be happy you must be prepared to explain your relationship to unhappiness. Then you will find that happiness is something that is cut off from or at the expense of its connection to other things. So, true happiness must recognise unhappiness.

VALUES

The concept of value underpins modern ethics. It seems to have emerged in response to the collapse of absolutes, universals and transcendental authority. The faster the rate of change the more dramatic has become the rise of values as arbiters of all things moral, ethical, social, political, ideological, and much besides. However, at the very core of modernity lies a much more straightforward notion, rendering arbitration unnecessary, namely the idea of uncovering, discovering, unravelling, or sheer emergence. Once the shackles of tradition were removed, actual being and the uninterrupted flow of becoming were made possible on an unprecedented scale, arguably for the first time in human history. It is no coincidence that such concepts as authenticity and freedom have moved to centre-stage in philosophical thinking – as a manifestation of the zeitgeist – but more to the point, as an expression of the now-liberated human spirit at large. Thus, to be free is to know thyself; to emerge as a fully-fledged individual is to actualise authentic existence; and to discover consciousness is to find one's worth.

It is this notion of worth that seems to be missing from the tyrannical rule of value. For, when one is aware, cognisant, conscious, and thereby conscientious, a self-sustaining authority acts as a guide and compass, rendering arbitration by values obsolete. It might be said that the idea of worth is the modern equivalent of the overarching classical idea of harmony, where everyone found their place in the grand scheme of things according to who they were. However, while knowing who you were in antiquity might have been decided by your class, gender, relationship or otherwise, it is the emergence of discovery, long sought-after and perceptibly-identified at the core of all things by Plato himself, that presents itself now as a universal within reach of everyone. Potential and possibility are the hallmarks of worth and, to paraphrase Sartre, we are condemned to have self-worth, the absence of which is but a manifestation of bad faith.

KNOWLEDGE

What is knowledge in the grand scheme of things? We are said to have entered a 'knowledge-based' era. Of course we can say that knowledge is an essential component of reality, that its roots are in metaphysics, and that it uses itself initially to substantiate concepts. And furthermore, as a property, mode and attribute of reality a la Spinoza, it helps us to explore our intuitions about reality.

But this doesn't get us very far. For all these claims assume that we, the speaker, writer or observer are at the centre of things, not that reality occupies that place. To put ourselves at the centre is an error. To appreciate knowledge fully we have to change the question - instead of asking if we know reality we can ask instead how knowledge gets us closer to reality or how we can evolve concepts that put us more in touch with it. Indeed, at the heart of knowledge lies the absolute. Socrates said that we know reality already but have forgotten it. For this reason classical philosophy does not go in search of reality but reveals that it is there already. Philosophy is in this sense not an academic discipline, that is to say a ring-fencing of verifiable knowledge, possessing its own methods. Philosophy occupies the space or the tension between people and the absolute. It relates to the idea of method, not to any particular method.

Thus it cannot be stressed too highly that the Holy Grail is reality, not knowledge. Derrida pointed out that to ask if we can know reality is to obfuscate a process that can only be followed if we ask how knowledge as a concept is helpful. Obviously knowledge is helpful up to a point;

knowledge is no different from reason in being a tool. But it is different from reality. How far then can the concept of knowledge help us in our search? At which point does it get replaced by other concepts? We must be careful in answering, for knowledge has acquired a distinct status. Yet, it is there to serve; it is not an end in itself. It has to be discarded if it ceases to serve its purpose.

Reality is not self-aware; it just is. Hence mind is a problematic notion. Indeed the myth of the Garden of Eden is telling us something. To know may carry the risk of losing touch with reality. The warning is there, loud and clear, not as a religious or moral admonition but primarily as a philosophical statement. To know is to split knower from known. Moreover, it introduces doubt, the flipside of knowledge. The Socratic journey of knowledge ends with the dictum 'I know that I don't know' – a double-take on a non-concept, a traversal of a thought-experiment, ending in annulment. Indeed, it might be argued that Plato stole Zeus' thunder from Socrates, raising an edifice of knowledge (episteme) on (or instead of) the foundations of being, living and philosophical conversation. Famously Plato went on to establish the Academy, a prototype of academe for millennia to come. He erected walls around the idea of knowledge and thus separated it from reality.

Thence the fiction of the ivory tower has come to replace reality in the simulacrum or matrix emerging from Plato. It was reinforced by the Neo-Platonists, and by Kant, with his foregrounding of phenomena and relegation of the noumena. All this follows from placing knowledge at the heart of philosophical thinking. Where academic 'knowledge' is taking us is a matter for debate. Suffice it to say that in popular parlance – the ultimate judge and jury of thought - the notion of 'academic' is not only used in opposition to reality but also as a caricature of knowledge itself. Indeed, the Hellenistic period is a desperate attempt to rescue Socrates from the Platonic grip of knowledge, resurrecting philosophy's emphasis on the lived-life and, beyond it, the idea of reality, within which life can be pursued.

By refusing to let reality be total we have created a redoubtable problem of how to validate knowledge. Knowledge has lost its status by slipping from ontology into the philosophy of mind and of meaning. It has virtually become the preserve of psychology. It is no longer a valid objection to any claim because there is no knowledge outside meaning. The question 'How do we know? has been universalised a la Kant. It is now a tedious question because knowledge is not considered adequate to the task. The components of knowledge are debunked, as is knowledge as a concept.

Two and a half millennia of obsession with knowledge have pushed the concept from its central position in philosophy. These days knowledge is relegated to the disciplines of linguistics and psychology, awaiting their deliberations and research. Not a day too soon, it might be said. Knowledge is a mind-property as well as a cultural (language) phenomenon. It pertains to the one who sets out to know and this knowledge-seeker may well project him- or herself into its areas of study. Knowledge is nothing less than an aggressive act of imposition, an act of anthropomorphism, an attempt to elevate mind to the level of reality. It is a retreat from philosophical monism, where everything (including mind) is but a part of the whole. We will return to mind and to the related question of personhood when dealing with the socio in the next chapter. For now, the attempt to address reality should focus our attention on reality and on it alone.

So, how should we read the Apollonian motto 'know thyself'? Is it an invitation for the knower to return to the known? Is it a closing of the gap that resulted from the emergence of mind so that attention could shift back to the pressing issue of the nature of things and of reality itself? Could it be that Plato missed the irony of Apollo, meant merely as a preliminary invocation to address oneself as a house-clearing, tool-laying, machine-oiling necessity? Was Apollo preparing us for the task of facing outwards so we could connect with reality as a whole? Is 'know thyself' a therapeutic exercise? Or is it a healing device, an invitation to meditation, a person-centred, mind-focused, awareness-raising recipe, taken beyond its remit?

SUMMARY

We have found that these three palliatives fail to create or reveal harmony. What then does it mean *to be,* completely devoted to presence and immanence, exempt from doing, devoid of consciousness and its endless derivatives? How can we conceptualise the serenity, the equanimity, the patience of waiting? Socrates advises us to clear the rubble. Plato invokes the metaphor of a piece of sculpture emerging as the sculptor chips away at a block of marble. The Sceptics knocked down any permanence of thought. Indeed, philosophy is devoted to asking questions in a search for that which can be addressed. Arguably, the philosophical canon emerges as a long-term exercise in preparation. For, to face reality requires a kind of attention which is otherwise missing or not available in the hurly-burly of life. To 'be' is thus, philosophically speaking, a projected end or goal of the entire philosophical project. So, either there is a paradox at the heart of philosophy, which elevates thought over being, whilst knowing all along that the latter is the sole justification of the former, or else we have misunderstood the nature of philosophy. When Karen Armstrong invites us to consider both Buddhism and Hellenism as emanating from the same source she may well be on to something. For the emptying of the mind as advocated by the Buddha is also the purpose of classical philosophy. Both resonate with the contemporary notion of mindfulness as a euphemism for clearing the mind. An interesting conclusion might be that, far from raising consciousness or increasing awareness, the aim of philosophy is to throw away our way-pointers and to expose the pitfalls and minefields of 'being aware.' This phrase is a potential oxymoron, the invocation of which goes counter to the placing of being as an end in and of itself.

We describe reality as if we stand outside it. The truth is we are both inside and outside at the same time. Our mind tells us that we can stand outside it at the same time that it tells us that there is nothing apart from what mind comprehends. Yet we are always immersed in reality, regardless of the constructs our mind throws up in an attempt to define and contain it.

Only by accepting our total immersion can we take ourselves to be an integral part of the whole.

It is a failure of thinking to suppose we are totally connected in reality, as Buddhism seems to suggest. Freud said that we are unable to know ourselves, and we can extrapolate from this claim and say that we cannot fully know reality. In our inmost self we know we don't know. It is both obvious and trivial to say our mind cannot know itself. We can 'know' reality only as a concept. The concept of reality already grasps something. And this something is not available when we accept Descartes' claim that mind, the Cogito, can break away from reality. Our appreciation of knowledge breaks down; for reality knows; it is 'in the know' in a way that mind can never provide for us.

So, what can we do about the idea of mind? The question has still to be asked: does mind serve as a good analogy, metaphor or signification for reality itself, given that the former is a constituent element of the latter? If mind does serve this purpose, does this mean that reality is aware? It is indeed difficult to conceive of reality being capable of the act of self-awareness, or even of possessing the very inclination to be aware in the first place. It is not that awareness is missing from its tapestry.

Rather, it is imbued or imprinted, as it were, in its very fabric. For awareness is a property of being, as are all mind-dependent properties, a given so to speak, taken for granted, assimilated into the whole. One might say by way of analogy that whilst awareness is embedded in reality in the fullest sense of the word, reality does not concern itself with the property of mind that registers, categorises, measures, and reflects. In short, it is not obsessed with itself. Reality just is, to repeat the cliché. It is not seeking to know itself, because it already knows.

Some general conclusions can be drawn about mind as a property of reality. Firstly, the properties of all constituents of reality apply to reality itself. The parts are indicative of the whole. Secondly, while the parts seek to relate to one another (knowledge as relationship), the whole contains all relationships within itself. Thirdly, the integration within reality of that which is separate in its constituent parts signals a Gestalt transformation, where the sum is more than its parts. Fourthly, it can be argued that philosophy is a discipline applicable to the study of wholes or totalities, where the otherwise explicit is inherently implicit. A game-change is thus called for, where thought amounts to observation and *a priori* knowledge. So, reality is an archetypal concept of manifestation and thinking, leading to recognition, acceptance, (re)discovery, emergence of harmony (where all the parts know themselves whilst knowing their place in the great scheme of things) and the autonomy of congruent completeness.

What then, in conclusion, should be done about mind as an idea? Firstly, the best outcome might be its wholesale relegation - lock, stock and barrel – to psychology. In the same way that science has come to inherit natural philosophy, to the extent that the term no longer carries conviction, the same is now happening in front of our eyes elsewhere. The whole realm of the human (including consciousness and mind) is joining up with natural science or emerging as a different 'science' (episteme, knowledge) alongside the natural one. It is not inconceivable that what we know as science today will multiply into sciences in the plural, where all phenomena will be addressed in their own and proper context. Indeed, the correspondence between psychology and the properties of the mind is now almost complete.

Secondly, it is possible to conceive of a redress of mind and its intricacies back to a (meta)physical context where mind is but a manifestation, however dazzling it may be, of the disposition of the observer. That is to say, the riddle of the mind as both observer and observed can be put to rest by collapsing observer into the observed and realising at the same time that it is but an infinite regress. Thus we can accept that we always see ourselves through others' eyes. The deconstruction of mind paves the way for the reconstruction of reality, and with it the renewal of metaphysics. The operation of mind is well-enough understood. Now we must look at something else – the socio – that, it is becoming apparent, infiltrated mind from the outset and possesses even greater power to hold reality at bay.

SECTION THREE: THE SOCIO

CHAPTER EIGHT - WHAT IS THE SOCIO?

So far I've argued that the mind has penetrated everywhere except metaphysics, philosophical method and the body. I will argue below (Chapters Twelve to Fifteen) that these aspects of philosophy are still capable of rising to the challenge of mind. But before that we must take note of something that can be sensed behind mind; and something incomparably more powerful, far-reaching and difficult to identify than mind. The previous chapters have argued that the causes of the mind-reality quandary are now well-enough understood for the issue of mind to be laid aside. Yet human suffering will not go away. People are unable to make a clean contact with each other. I will put the case in this and the next chapter that, though this is caused by forces presently beyond our understanding, ideas can nonetheless be advanced. In brief, I argue that, because we emerged from the savannah in packs, human beings have never fully engaged with reality. This is to do with the nature of human aggregation. Reality always looms; yet, as it does we become afraid of it. We do this because the mind has detached itself from the body. Then we turn to morals or alcohol because reality seems too stark. We try to sweeten the horror by distancing ourselves. So, our engagement is never more than partial.

I

The socio, it has to be said at the outset, lies beyond issues of free will, intentionality, authenticity, performative self-consciousness; of evolution or psychology. The socio is a totality, or an immensely powerful simulacrum of one. Where other explanations invoke oppression by a powerful force such as language, social order, or childhood experiences, the socio I argue has replaced mind as the way of configuring reality. However, something more seems to be happening – the possibility cannot be dismissed that the socio is built into the very nature of human aggregation. It doesn't arise in opposition to authority but is rather an effect of attraction. It is akin to Deleuze's 'assemblages,' yet, because of its power to make individuals feel comfortable with each other and at the same time to keep reality at bay, it possesses features of both his plane of organisation and plane of immanence. It thus begs new thinking. In that this force operates as a totality only metaphysics and philosophical method possess the appropriate tools and scale to open the issue up. We are faced with the prospect of failure if we attempt to define the blockage to our engagement with reality using dualist, logical or propositional thinking. Each branch of philosophy, except metaphysics and philosophical method, leads us immediately to mind-constructs. Canonical and current thinking have gone too far down this road to provide a viable totalising approach. The problem is not that things originate in the mind or, as Kant claimed, mind imposes itself on reality. It is even worse than that, for the mind itself is a construct of thinking. One of my themes up to this point is that mind is unnecessary – it is an ordering process after all that has evolved as a buffer against reality. It can be trusted as a source of knowledge only when what is known is collapsed into what is unknown. Yet current thinking is still dominantly in thrall to it. Mind is not a totality; it is only an idea, the application of which still leaves it as a small part of reality. In contrast, the socio is a totality. In an as yet unascertainable way reality appears to have used or allowed the socio to create mind, making the socio the best approximation to reality. To focus on the way the mind has created riddles for us to unravel is to miss the point. The view from under the aspect of eternity is the only one that offers a way forward.

Many commentators have gained a sense of a pervasive, universal force that makes people act against their natural interest, from Orwell's 'Reality control,' 'Newspeak' and 'doublethink' to McLuhan's 'The Medium is the Message;' from Heidegger's 'Das Man' to Deleuze's 'good sense' and Lacan's 'Big Other,' 'Symbolic Order,' and 'Master Signifier.' But these ideas have failed to recognise that the mind which produced them is only a phenomenon. Indeed, the mind is only a third move behind reality, the socio being the second. Why then should we claim the power to address reality as if it lies 'beyond,' in the way that mind tells us, when the idea of 'beyond' is itself a construct of a bifurcating mind? When however we take the world as our sole referent these ideas can be seen as misrecognitions. I return to the Greek notion: we are already real when we clear from our thinking the many accretions of mind-debris that stop us recognising that we are already real. We have a choice; accept what the mind has constructed- such as desire and language - and then explain how this affects life, or, like the Greeks, abandon the mind that orders thought and produces constructs like desire or language. Yet, once we abandon mind we encounter the socio where we might have expected to engage with reality. It now remains for us to understand the socio's claim to be an approximation or simulacrum of totality.

II

The search for first principles has long been seen as a search for an end to suffering. The search for what is indivisible goes back to the Pre-Socratics. There has been no subsequent revolution (except perhaps in content) – 'all is water' now merely appears as 'all is the socio.' So a definition of the socio must firstly take account of its indivisibility and secondly explain the connection of this indivisibility to human suffering. As the socio is only just emerging into sight definitions cannot be exact. Its emergence can be essayed broadly however. My argument goes like this: Plato's underlying monism did not threaten the integrity of the true nature of its parts. Each part possesses the capacity to be a microcosm of the whole. But this is where things become complicated because Plato did not fully grasp the implications of his own ideas. This led him to fail to discern the socio. Thus, an individual begins to see the macrocosm and indivisibility of the socio within themselves at the same time that they see the other as microcosmic and indivisible. However, and this is the radical second move that confounds the first, yet another, countervailing, movement occurs at the same time. Indivisibility gives way to divisibility as the part becomes self-knowing. Kant told us that organisms are themselves multiplicities. An entity reveals its multiplicity as its self-knowledge grows. When for example groups of footballers, homosexuals or Christians gather together and become more aware of themselves as individuals, the category that initially described them and brought them together begins to reveal internal distinctions. Thus the individual sees how much commonality exists with others at the same time that he notices his separateness.

So, the abiding feature of the socio is that it is divisible and indivisible *at the same time*. The result is that, when the mind encounters a particular, it slips into a clearly defined, monolithic relationship to it, rather than dancing with it. This is a peculiar situation, for at this point individuals see themselves reflected in the other while also seeing the other as different – at one and the same time. Individuals appear to be able to handle either eventuality alone but not both at the same time. The first question to arise for the individual is: If the other is so different *and* so similar to me, who am I? The socio is a response to this confusion: it is an attempt to relieve distress and impose order.

I could of course have replied to a question about the definition of the socio by associating it with the promise of perfection that epistemology offers. And certainly the appeal of epistemology as a search for an origin shows us how seductive is the mind to philosophers in general. But the epistemology-ontology divide is the very thinking that I wish to avoid, because it takes us to a mind-dictated classification of 'everything' riven by splits, whereas I point to reality as the benchmark, not mind. When we privilege mind we must inevitably ask about everything systematically; in other words, we ask about that which presents itself to the mind. Yet here my starting point is philosophy as life itself, reality or totality. This is encompassed in the phrase 'everything that there is,' and I have explained how radically different this is from 'everything' in Chapter Two. My claim is that there is nothing but the philosophical search, that reality is a given, that we operate within it, and that there is nowhere we can rest our weary head in the realms of mind-projection. If we settle at some point on a question, answer, outcome, theory or concept we are not being truly philosophical. Philosophy is aware that some things emerge and others don't. It leaves all options open when reality is the benchmark. To think about everything in the way of Kant is to settle on or in the question; philosophy goes into a question and then through it and out the other side to another question. This is a crucial distinction. Philosophy holds up the present question to further questioning. It realises that all possibilities and alternatives are open, infinitely so; seeking any kind of incontrovertible answer is to be in thrall to the tendency of mind to want to capture that which it focuses on. One has to concede that the way we usually use mind does not encompass the totality of mind. If we focus on the totality of mind as the originator of things and take our thoughts away from Plato and his specific claims then it becomes clear that mind itself must have emerged from something bigger. Mind has untapped potential.

I want to look more deeply into this moment by claiming that the socio arises when we treat our proximity to fellow human beings as a matter of inordinate suffering. In terms of this encounter I can say that distress arises when an entity or individual attempts to bring to a halt the dance with the other. By imposing a closure on the undefined possibilities in the moment of encounter the individual will circumscribe the nature of the subsequent relationship. The opposite also applies: the longer an individual delays coming to a conclusion about the other the more the meeting will remain a matter of wonder and possibility. This is a bold claim; some may say a heartless one. Yet it does not deny suffering or the plight of others. Of course these areas of suffering - be they loss, conflict, guilt, sorrow, despair – are the very areas that other disciplines address. But philosophy asks more (not less) of these issues than the social sciences or medicine because it takes us to the unfolding difficulty of being alive. This may not relieve suffering in the short term, but it is certainly more practical in the longer term because it makes sure that unsubstantiated claims are not repeated.

Yet why would an individual curtail the dance and reject the possibilities of an enriched and compelling interaction? My suggestion, grounded in Platonic thinking, is that we become victims of society's fear of reality before we draw our first breath. Our parents, and theirs, schools, workplace and friends pass on so much defensive, regularised thinking to us that we deign to leave Plato's Cave. The socio offers an immediate, frictionless connection to the other that weakens our natural drive to be free and to connect freely. As we collapse under layers of accreted thinking we are promised absolution from a growing sense of bad faith. Even if it may be that the suffering caused by our abiding in the prison of accepted thinking is manageable, it is difficult to deny that some appreciable suffering accrues from knowing that we are complicit. Here the effect of the socio on human suffering approaches Heidegger's description of das Man and Lacan's Big Other and Symbolic Order. Das Man is an oppressive force that draws individuals into seeking peer acceptance.

Similarly, Lacan's Big Other and Symbolic Order operate under the stifling aegis of language. Yet both ideas are products of the dichotomising mind, whereas my claim for the socio is that it approximates to totality. In any case, the socio precedes or arises at the same time as the mind; it is not an outcome of it. Thus, the socio is not concerned with issues of subject-formation, desire-fuelled libidinal forces or the authority of the Oedipal father. Mind is only a part of the world. There is something pre-mind about the socio. Its vantage-point is the world. We need new concepts and terms to address it.

III

As a starting point I suggest the socio is a gene, meme or virus that seems to have imposed itself on all intellectual pursuits. At first it might appear to be an unnecessary add-on to reality, in the way that Lacan talks of reason being a parasite. The greatest irony is that the faculty to which we would look for help – the enquiring mind – is itself both incubator and transmitter. Even reality's totality is challenged by the socio! Can there be two totalities? It infects all communities of thought. For example, scientism is a community of scientists that has been corrupted by the socio. Peer pressure ensures that nothing is deemed to be an addition to knowledge unless it is subjected to peer-review. Thus, radical divergence from the mean is viewed with acute suspicion. The socio induces in us an acceptance of this all-pervasive, subtle disposition to the extent that we persuade ourselves that our corrupted thoughts are real. Yet we are left at an inexplicable angle to reality; we are satisfied superficially while at the same time feel deeply out of sorts. Life seems to be split into all kinds of dichotomies; we feel it necessary to resolve these splits or to champion one side of the divide against the other.

So, while promising to relieve anxiety, the socio perpetuates it. Out of the split and the resulting anxiety ethics grows. We cannot long deny reality: madness and misery are an inevitable result. The socio seems to sustain a fragile attempt at wholeness in the face of absolute totality. Energy is taken up and anxiety generated in sustaining the belief that completion will be attained when we reach the desired object and close the gap that keeps it out of reach. Yet, epistemology's desire to centre or fix things is an unnecessary move. When we follow the Greek idea that reality is always already here, then we see that striving is unnecessary and we should stop trying. Spinoza expressed this point as a need only to think adequately. The prisoners in Plato's cave might be said to be prisoners to over-thinking, their torpor the result of exhaustion rather than stupidity or lack of thought.

The socio enables us to avoid facing the truth. Instead we live in a half-world. In the sense that Jesus died in the name of truth or reality, the socio keeps this prospect at bay; we need no longer go all the way and risk following his fate. We avoid taking full responsibility for our true nature. We never allow ourselves to do anything fully for fear of being criticised, shunned or punished. The socio is thus more insidious and more difficult to describe than mind, morality, social conformity or the generation of desire as outlined by Heidegger, Lacan or Deleuze. It claims to be reality with a power and pervasiveness that makes us blind to reality itself. The Greeks thought that reality was revealed when the mind was expanded until it corresponded with reality. At that point we could trust the mind or (in effect, the same thing) abolish it. We now see that the socio early began to undermine Greek thinking. The philosophical canon tells us that Plato's first move in his search for reality took him to mind. And until recently mind has been seen as the problem, the self-proclaimed arbiter of reality, a part of the universe that claims to represent the whole. Now we can see that the Platonic project substantially failed to trace the socio lurking with such strength both within and as an alternative to reality, and to see that mind was already a secondary problem.

We think of mind as 'ours.' Yet when we speak we invariably express the socio in the form of *vox populi* and then pass this off as an outcome of mind. Hidden assumptions seep into what we think and say. What we express comes over as a move towards multiplicity, a willingness to curb ourselves in order to rub along with others. Society seeks this accommodation, fearing that members of groups will otherwise turn to narcissistic satisfaction. Thus, by default, administrative thinking happened upon a great truth. The multiplicity and plurality that civil society seeks as an administrative goal are there at the origin, at the very heart of connectivity. Loving bonds between people and support within communities have been hailed as the answer to the fragmentation of modern life. Yet, I argue, connectivity itself has gone seriously astray. We can now see that the socio represents itself as the sum total of reality. Emerging within the process of connectivity, it even confounds connectivity.

The socio tells us with unaccounted authority where everything hails from. It is there at the origin of things, in the most intimate and raw situations. It is there even as things interact and relationships form. It is found even as potential, being revealed in creativity and in love for instance. Entities discover they possess alien, inexplicable aspects of themselves. There are so many words for an aggregative force: flock, tribe, nation, or mob. It is a composite that we do not want to look at. Yet, groups do not need to introduce diversity in order to co-exist; each group already possesses diversity at its core, expressed as fertility, potentiality, excess, or untapped ripeness. Yet, when all is said and done, the socio has not subsumed reality; any claim to ontological status rests only with reality itself.

The socio is not an untrue or diluted version of reality or a turn away from it. The nearest definition is a copy or simulacrum. If for example we were to strip the socio away from the arts, the self or from society it would be impossible at present to say what would be left. We are rarely asked to view things in general unless we adjust our understanding to make allowance for such concepts or presuppositions as utility, rights, values, relevance or ethics. In a world where everything is an application ('app') to something else, to a point where the original is virtually ignored, reality has disappeared from sight. Reality and truth appear prominently now only in crime fiction where the detective and a forensic scientist strive to prove the guilt of a suspect. Otherwise simulacra reign supreme.

Everyone gains from the application of science to technology at the level of the simulacrum, beyond differences of wealth, education, culture, class, or attitude, in a seamless process that equalises us all as consumers. We are told that the sublime is attainable by reading a novel, attending a musical concert or applying the insights of social science to our lives. The application is king and everything is hunky-dory.

Life becomes a wearing struggle against an unseen manipulator a la Kafka and Dostoevsky. Critics of postmodernism point to the loss of universal thought that was previously afforded by God. Human organisms are free initially, but are quickly drawn together into a web of obligations and roles that they associate with consciousness. But consciousness is weak and the attainment of independent thought is an arduous process. Obligations and roles based on a sense of comradeship that derives from the socio are difficult to bypass. Consciousness may have arisen as a defence against the starkness and rawness of reality. However, in its weakness it leaves a gap between it and reality. Here the socio enters as a much stronger force with the power to soften the sharp edges of reality. We now become persuaded we are cared for. A kind of pseudo-connection to others obtains in this penumbra of reality that keeps at bay the apparent coldness and meaninglessness of existence. Soldiers are said to develop comradeship that sustains them in battle as a more powerful motivating force than military authority, nationalism or sectarianism. Yet this web of roles and obligations seems to have grown alongside consciousness. It creates a sense of connectedness that precedes the recruitment of men by the military authorities.

III

The socio is found in and emerges from an idea. For example, once the Nazis claimed that Jews, gays and gypsies were bad; this claim then seemed to warrant little serious further consideration. Mob formation is underpinned by organising principles, despite the fear of others that they represent chaos. The mob's intellectualising is a reaction against what it itself sees as dangerous and unorganised. It claims to have identified a self-evident truth. All intellectual movement is then taken over and given a new direction. And yet ironically reality operates through the socio. Madness is a case in point. If the mad are seen as those least able to submit to the constrictions of the socio, their behaviour has nonetheless to be addressed by the socio. They may be incarcerated, but even then the mad are granted rights to oppose what are seen as the most extreme manifestations of the socio, unlimited incarceration for instance. The socio claims to solve the problem it itself has created. Just as capitalism incorporates all those movements and ideas that challenge it, so the socio has to double back on itself in an act of self-preservation. This is a manoeuvre that can be revealed with a moment's thought, yet society seems fearful of going there for fear that the whole thought system would collapse. The result is of course that a person can no longer be authentic in the way that Nietzsche advocated.

We can start by looking at what happens to things in the world. There is no purpose or organising principle in nature, as there is no aimlessness or evil behind it. Drives originate in recognition, love, and the bundling of activities into the categories of in or out. From this bundling there emerge sets of rules that differentiate those who accept the parameters and those who don't. Despite the apparent march of history yielding liberation, human rights and so on, it is *vox res* that rules, not *vox populi*! However, in the midst of everything, philosophy refuses to be partial or binary and seeks a principle that explains everything. It recognises that it is not individual freedom that moves the universe but the forces of aggregation. The socio relates to these philosophical developments because they are responsive to each other; they exist, are created or emerge in bundles.

The socio plays on a wish to be a member of an amorphous majority. The wish to belong or be loved seems to emerge from a belief that others know something more about the universe or about us than we do. Thus, when we are told we benefit by dichotomising or separating entities – self from society, self from other, knowledge from ignorance, good from bad, civilisation from barbarity – we see that our best interest lies in conformity to one side. This move is close to Kant's definition of radical evil, which makes sense on the level of simple survival. But, in the spirit of this book and taking it that you the reader have got this far, you are being asked to abandon self-interest and become a philosopher. Nonetheless the argument for conformity goes - it is better to be good, knowledgeable or civilised than to be bad, ignorant or barbarous. Indeed, in this way we will join an august community of the good, knowledgeable and civilised. We have found a home of like-minded people, a community that in effect supports the same football team. This thinking is the socio manifesting itself. Yet, its emergence does nothing but confuse matters. If we take the manifestation of the socio in capitalism as an example it becomes clear that such seemingly pure expressions of the human spirit as love, care, and radical thinking have been taken over by consumer advertising. Love sells cars; care is tied to health insurance; and radical thinking is portrayed as a characteristic of new technology that helps sell the latest model of mobile phone. A sense of common ground has appeared that universalises enlightenment; increased consumption and saturated advertising are said to promote all the things we are told are good.

The socio reveals itself when we recognise our fellow beings or accept the common ground between us. What is this but a way of describing Plato's theory of Forms? Yet, we are attracted to or fall in love with each other so easily that it seems paradoxical to stress the common source. Einstein claimed that four forces help us to understand the world better than molecular or atomic theories. We do not need to move towards each other for support, defence or attraction; we are connected, at one, already. We deny this when we seek to actualise our being. Heidegger jumped the gun when he said the problem is in the singular. We are all pluralities at the outset, as Heraclitus told us. By going towards each other we become parts of others in networks of multiplicities a la Deleuze: clouds of the virtual interact long before the actual comes into close proximity. We need to know more about what it means for us to be connected *a priori* so we can understand the nature of 'group-think.'

IV

It would be easy to explain this situation in terms of the mind. Yet it is the socio that colonises every aspect of reality; it has infiltrated mind. This is not to claim that some physical or neurological malfunctioning is impairing the mind; rather, that the mind is not consistently pure. In an agitated state it cannot conceive the big picture. Kant tells us that pure reason creates categories such as time and space. Yet, what the mind understands when it operates in this way has nothing to do with its range of capabilities; rather it has to do with the channels along which the socio has guided it. No longer is philosophy (with the exception of metaphysics) a reliable entry point into enquiry. It cannot be stressed enough that even as we investigate the socio we generate it. Nonetheless it doesn't emanate from the soul or human intention but from process itself. This is why philosophical method alone is capable of investigating it. Pandora and all other myths suggest that wonder and curiosity open doors that cannot then be closed. It doesn't matter whether the impulse was intentional or not. The socio is not otherworldly, nor is it the Devil or reality. It is generated in the very process of investigation. Research contains a kind of radioactivity that ends up polluting the search.

There is something of the socio in the gibe that do-gooders cause more harm than good. Ironically, we suffer from our excess. Once we make the transfixing move into love, relationship, caring, acquiring insights or wisdom – in other words, having our minds opened to reality – we pay a price for finding the truth, a price in the form of the corruption of our blessed state. Process, motion and throughput are the world as thing-in-itself. Process is not structural and therefore cannot be defined as a cause, and yet ironically the generation of the socio lies in process.

The socio can be described as creating a nexus between people that takes away their authenticity. If we separate the investigator from the investigation we can focus on the investigator as thing-in-itself and thus take the investigation to be the product of his or her mind. This we can suppose will open the person to the anxiety that Paul Tillich has written about. He posits two routes thereafter: to the universe or to the individual. The individual can appear as a temporary framing of questions that loom large as we move towards the universal route. The universal route can only be taken with a 'courage to be' once all crutches of the apparent world fall away.

Because the old questions about philosophy are contaminated by the socio we must ask questions about the previous investigations themselves. And then ask where a question arises from – a disturbance for instance. If so, we can assume that the question itself contributed to the disturbance. This is Whitehead's idea of an expansive reality. Another level of reality might appear and then we must peel it away, ad infinitum. The old questions will gain new life. We become beneficiaries as we realise that reality in conjunction with our investigation has created a new philosophy. More subtle questions can be asked of social concepts like crime, where the splitting of good from bad misses the point. The capacity of the socio is great enough to bring perpetrator and victim together in an intricate web of connections that confounds them as ethical markers. Metaphysics is the only method that can question everything thoroughly. We need it to identify claims to reality that otherwise are the socio in disguise. Certainly, reality includes what human have created but we must ask: does philosophy have to include what humans have created *as a part of the structure of reality?*

In the preceding pages I have presented two propositions. One: reality is all there is. Two: the socio is all around and in us. This leaves a gap or difference that is revealed in the relation of the 'is' to the 'us.' In short, reality exists while the socio is only felt or perceived. We betray ourselves when we put perspective before being. The effect is that the 'all' is compromised. Confusingly, it now assumes more than one meaning. To the extent that we validate felt experiences we compromise reality. There is now no 'is' but instead a contaminated 'all.' Reality has given way to a belief in a personal reality that is itself produced by social pressures.

CHAPTER NINE - THE SOCIO: AGGREGATION AND THE NATURE OF ENTITIES

The questions we have to ask are: what is an entity? and: what happens when an entity connects to multiplicities or aggregations? As indicated in the previous chapter, the work of Nietzsche, Deleuze and others tells us that entities are relationships that are open to internal and external flows. Nothing about them is fixed. We are now able both to distinguish between difference and identity and understand better the nature of discreteness and the relation between entities. The discreteness of an entity is relational and proximate. Take the idea of a journey as an example of the relation of the particular to the whole. A moving train can be observed from the traveller's constantly changing point of view or from an external observer's location at one point along the journey. From the traveller's point of view there can be no single instance of difference of speed; everything is local, comparative and affective. What might appear as differences of speed are in fact portions of the traveller's journey, not points on the journey itself. A similar perspectival dissonance arises with regard to blockages and overflows of energy. Deleuze points to difference being a matter of intensities not categories. His idea of 'the actualisation of the virtual tendencies' describes the overflow onto surrounding territory of energy blocked in an entity as its identity hardens.(1) Nietzsche suggests that, in a state of immanence, ever-changing forces will affirm their difference from other forces. Active forces go to the limit of what they can do; reactive forces limit what both they and active forces can do. Yet, when reactive forces take the ascendant, or transcendental positions are created, difference retreats and identity ossifies, or so it would appear. Not so, says Deleuze, space will fracture in this instance; the environs of an ossification of identity will receive an overflow of the entity's energy. Forces that have been contained will seek to breech their limit. Whether they become active or reactive is the key point, for Nietzsche's reactive force is what comes closest to what I am calling the socio. An overflow of energy causes aggregation; the resulting fear drives entities to harden their identity and prevent reality passing through them. Instead, energy is displaced onto surrounding entities. In this sense a crowd or a mob may not have a single ideology but the pressures that drove people to them are questions of identity, thus requiring some level of internal assembly of ideas.

I

Aggregation is an answer to the problems thrown up by dichotomised thinking. The ideas in the earlier section on Logic apply to the socio. In contradistinction to what logic tells us, opposites are not mutually-exclusive. They can attract each other. Aggregation presents us with a non-logical relationship between apparent opposites that can lead to union between opposites or to the appearance of a meta-concept that will embrace both sides of a divide. (2)

Rosenzweig argues that the problem of aggregation arises in the changing relation of the particular to the universal. (3) The particular is without movement and therefore direction; the universal is passive but a force of attraction emanates from it. Things happen when the particular falls into the force-field of the universal. Noticing its movement in that direction it opens to its own nature with regard to the universal. It is now no longer merely a particular but a thing that is conscious of itself as a particularity. It has already reached the frontier where the power of the universal is exercised. It has reached a station on the road to the universal that reveals itself as an 'individual' particular, distinguished by being aware of its own nature. However, Rosenzweig sees this juncture as the place where problems might occur: the species, people, state, genus or community seek to insert him or her into their midst. The individual arises at birth but the genus appears in the coupling of individuals. These aggregations are 'unconditioned universalities' lacking an ontological foundation.

'Yet, this individuality is attracted with a dark violence by the power of its species; it moves towards this central point by always distancing itself from the day of its birth, full of all possibilities, with a constant loss of possibilities – within individuality; in order finally to renounce it as much as possible at the moment of coupling. In coupling, the individual has entered fully into the species, he who from the time of his birth was fully individual, practically like a thing, with neither connection nor relation, only touched by the concept and not by the reality of his species.' (4)

The species is the product of applied thinking to which individuals become joined by an 'and' (the individual and the species, the thing and its concept, man and his community). The individual is just beginning to emerge as the thing-in-itself, manifesting in movement and creativity; change and transformation; resonance and recognition, and then the call of the socio overtakes it. Flux between and within aggregates is thus the dynamic of an unrecognised socio. It appears when groups form and dialogue opens. It is the organising principle that mitigates the fear of unpredictability engendered when people assemble. It is most evident when appeals are made to law or arbitration. Spontaneity goes out of the window as the cry goes up: 'We must do something and not leave things to themselves.'

II

Discussion of 'other minds' posits a single mind looking out at the world and wondering if other beings have minds. This single mind (our own) observes our colleagues observing the world; they are, as part of my perceived, mind-created reality, outside my sense of self. I do not see them on my side of the divide, looking at reality viewing what I am viewing. The idea of the socio posits, not a single mind on one side of a divide and all else on the other, but all other minds on this side looking out. It assumes a convergence of minds, an acceptance of the idea of mind. Only because the socio is a claim to totality can we do this. The socio takes us from the particularity of mind to a pseudo-reality or pseudo-totality and away from reality per se.

We can place this assessment in the area of subjectivity. Descartes tells of a single mind that looks out on reality from one side of a divide. This schema begins to expand and change in subtle and profound ways when we consider not one mind but a community of minds. This community is the socio. At its core it has a mind but it also comprises many other minds. This is now a bigger, deeper concept than Descartes'. It tells us that, when the philosopher looks at the world, he or she accepts that others do too. The notion of mind becomes two minds and eventually all minds; they combine and relate to each other. All these minds might disagree about what they see yet in that disagreement there is love for each other, so much so that an expansion of each mind takes place. So, as one mind looks out at the world and appreciates another doing the same thing two enhanced minds emerge.

We can go further and make some assumptions about other minds. The other-minds discussion has until recently omitted the matter of relationship. Firstly, we can accept that others in relationship to us respond in the ways that we do; secondly, for this very reason, others will know our responses before we are conscious of responding. Relationship breaks down the illusion of a split between self and other. Thus relationship takes the matter to the level of metaphysics. Here we can either start to observe without being an observer, by responding without an ego or without feeling drawn to explain what is happening in terms of free will or agency. Or we can succumb to the socio.

The socio is the development of the concept of mind as it moves towards plurality. CS Lewis represents two minds looking out on the world as a symbol of friendship which he contrasts to two minds looking at, and getting lost in, each other as a symbol of love. (5) One is a sharing move between two discrete beings, the other a possessive one between two needy beings. The socio is the beginning of a move towards monism and reality. It closes the gap that appears in the traditional One-Many split. This split occurs when reality is seen from the vantage point of a single mind. Aggregation of minds sees things from the side of mind too but also sees the way that reality approaches mind. Reality can be expressed as plurality plus oneness. When we see reality as plurality we can see the way that mind seeks to aggregate it into the One. The Pre-Socratic ideas of the One and the Many have thrown up two problems. Firstly, the separation that occurs as one looks and then realises one is looking, thereby immediately creating a gap. The other arguably arises when the mind is seen as the One. Aggregated minds begin to replace the mind not with reality but with the socio.

Aggregation offers a non-logical relationship between apparent opposites that is neither an in-between nor a non-in-between. Rather, it is a dynamic, inclusive, creative interplay between what at first appear to be discrete entities. It throws up the implication that logic does not apply to certain areas of life.

The move of a single mind towards the socio as it aggregates with others has nothing to do with the epistemological question asked in discussions of 'other minds.' There the search is for evidence or reasoning to justify an assertion that there are minds other than one's own. That approach takes mind as the starting point. The idea of the socio starts from the vantage point of totality. It thus expands beyond the 'how' or 'why' of other-minds discourse to the 'is' of metaphysics. It can do this because the socio makes claims to totality, one that rivals reality. The difference however is that reality just is; the socio is all around. Reality exists, whereas the socio is only felt and processed. To the extent that we validate the socio we compromise reality.

SECTION FOUR: PHILOSOPHY PENETRATED

CHAPTER TEN - PHILOSOPHY PENETRATED, PART I

Mind penetrated philosophy at its birth. It is no wonder that a sense of wholeness has disappeared and that the pages of the cultured press no longer present philosophy as making a greater contribution to life than for example literature, science or religion. Natural philosophy and political philosophy, the children of the zeitgeist, are instead the first ports of call. This is not a puzzle when we realise that behind mind is the all-pervasive socio. It is no surprise that the heart of philosophy has been penetrated too. All branches of philosophy other than metaphysics have tried hubristically to make the part stand for the whole, and to make dualisms become an accepted pillar of critique. (1) In other words, self-consciousness entered philosophy and took us into a smaller realm than totality. The history of ideas reveals a slight but crucial veering away from reality as thought converges on it. Plato offered us the idea of origin – everything comes from a common source; Aristotle offered the idea of telos; Spinoza the will, and so on. These and other key ideas have been presented as a fulcrum or an underpinning of reality. Yet we can now see that all these key concepts are not sufficient; they do not begin to explain criminality or madness for instance. They take us only to the point where it can be argued that binary opposites attract – not merely as expressed by Heraclitus, but so too the Being of Heidegger and Sartre needs non-Being to attain totality. Nonetheless the collapse of absolutes is but the latest move that reveals how close philosophy stays to the vibes of social life. Indeed a glaring openness to social values is apparent in all significant ideas that divide and dichotomise. This is revealed for example in the belief that the difference between any two entities is greater than the difference within either one, and that Enlightenment reason shines much brighter than intuition and myth. On the one hand, as ideas blossom and dualisms melt away, we discover more and more reality and reality affects us more. This is true of monism where there is no oppositional attrition to exploit. But, on the other hand, because the socio offers itself as a healer of splits (though it cannot survive without them), it is uncritically seen to lie at the heart of things as a protector of freedom and a bulwark against barbarity. It operates by making an unfounded claim that persuades us that it is better (more constructive, more ameliorative) to go this way rather than that. Rarely is this directionality questioned.

The socio is there at the beginning of philosophy. Both Thales' contention that all is water and the world-force that Anaxagoras identifies as nous indicate its ubiquity. Parmenides and Heraclitus grappled with it; the discussion of the One and the Many is infused with it. The One recognises and needs the Many and the Many seek the One or Oneness. To find the origin of the socio, if we hold to the Greek idea of remembering, we must go back further than mind. Freud said that the baby is formed when language enters the baby in the first few months of its life; Melanie Klein said the baby is formed when the mother enters the baby.

Plato initially took his project to be the disencumbering of the individual soul, in acknowledgement of his debt to Socrates. Only in *Republic* and *Laws* did he finally uncover the socio. But he held back from firmly pronouncing on his discovery. Thus mind held prime position as the barrier to reality until Kant demonstrated its failure as a bridge to reality. Thence the power of mind (as reason) was effectively confined to epistemology. Mind can now be seen only to contemplate mind. But Heidegger took up Kant's challenge. For Heidegger, philosophy was about the return to source. Accordingly he expanded mind from its narrow Kantian definition by including the body. Moreover, he took the major step to broaden the definition of mind into a concept that totalised emergence. It totalised the experience of being in the world. Yet, although it was insufficient to the task, it did at least bring subject and object nearer to each other. And more than that, it recognised that a third existed in the area of subjectivity-objectivity, namely the intersubjective. Heidegger recognised that the socio resides where beings relate to each other as much as they relate to the world or to themselves. Yet he held back from total recognition. Plato took us almost the whole way, but Heidegger added to our understanding when he trenchantly described the socio (without yet knowing the concept) as 'being in the world.'

I

All branches of philosophy are an attempt to help us think about reality. Yet none is inherently a replacement for it. As AW Moore puts it, 'all branches are the philosophy of this or that and more pertinently the *study* of them.' (1)) Metaphysics is thinking about thinking about the nature of things, not the nature of thinking or studying of this or that particularity. The invitation is to return these branches to reality for, until now, all separate aspects of philosophy have beckoned us to the socio. Thinkers have become victims of their own wisdom. The more the socio is grasped the more it develops clever ways to by-pass surveillance. Philosophers have not been sufficiently aware that they have failed. They have been happy with sufficient ideas and failed to realise the scale of the challenge before them. Yes, the concepts of joy and of mind for example have improved the human lot. But philosophy has stopped there. Language is accepted as a barrier to expansive thinking because of the power of syntax. Friendship, connection and attraction reach out to us but we are told that mind gets in the way with its devious tricks. We want love, approval or altruism yet in our highest aspiration to be close to other people the socio consolidates itself. It is there in such diverse landmarks as the myth of the Fall and Lacan's mirror phase.

The reflexive capacity within reality that we call the mind is capable of convincing us that we can step out of the flux and process of totality. This happens most obviously when mind tells us reality is split into two segments – the 'I' or knowing subject on the one hand and everything else that the 'I' can know on the other. Dualist thinking of this kind throws up innumerable problems which are looked at in later chapters. It seems to be able to make the concept of reality as totality somehow irrelevant to our daily lives, where we live in the belief that we are discrete, even isolated, beings or selves. Yet, to live in this way can be said to be an underlying cause of all the ills of mankind.

Courage is needed as we deepen our thinking beyond this general point because the journey never stops. Every time we come to a halt we can realise we have succumbed to socio and mind. Yet, as energy is generated new ideas will emerge. Fresh questions arise when the first layer of thinking (that which upholds the philosophical canon) is subjected to a second level of enquiry. Incidentally, in so doing innumerable social assumptions will become clearer: to take just one example, the popularity of the NHS has meant that few attempts are made to challenge its definition of health primarily in physical terms.

Moreover, once groups or aggregations are established, they become hierarchized and accounted for by replicating an idea that is never fully explained. For instance, why do we obey the law when people are so varied? Uniformity is imposed on diversity. The result is that some of us then over-obey to the extent of rebelling. The five branches of philosophy seem to possess integrity. Yet, ethics is blind when issues like justice or empathy arise, the ostensible focus of its attention. It invites us to accept a form of intellectual commonality and thereby to repress our true expression. Epistemology is a study of, not an enquiry into, knowledge. We first need to enquire into what comprises knowledge. A form of propaganda is used to get us to believe we know it already in a particular way. This is the socio at work. To know is to be socialised. Political philosophy claims to be an enquiry into the workings of the State. It signally falls short because it operates on the basis of unacknowledged assumptions with a very narrow scope. Even anarchism is open to the insidiousness of the socio that in its debased form becomes politics. Aesthetics has become a socially-mediated discipline. At one extreme we are told we must appreciate it and agree it is a good thing if we wish to be civilised or cultured. At the other extreme aesthetics becomes relativist: *everything* is beautiful. The socio has replaced beauty with taste. Even the great ontology, the thing-in-itself, has succumbed. True enquiry must focus on something that cannot be separated from the enquiring mind. When we call this the thing-in-itself to exemplify the reach of mind we fail to appreciate that it is not free of the socio. The very nature of discourse or enquiry (perhaps because of the nature of language a la Kant and Wittgenstein) suffers from our inability to step outside them, to the point that it cannot proceed. Concepts such as truth or good have become aspects of the socio; Socrates and Plato were defeated in the very moment of their engagement with them. The reach of the socio within philosophy is all but total.

II

By putting reality aside for the moment in the next chapter we can look at the way the human mind has constructed reality. I illustrate this development by looking at four of the five branches of philosophy (leaving metaphysics to Chapter Twelve); the four explanations; three epistemologies; and Plato's three ontologies. All these areas have given us trenchant insights into philosophy. All are however trammelled by binary thinking. The irony is that the search for truth, which constitutes the philosophical canon, tells the reader where to find compromised thinking. As we look more closely into those ideas we can see the way individual great minds have slipped into conformity with the zeitgeist. Socrates accepted death; Plato privileged the Good; Aristotle the mean; Neo Platonists - the One; starting with scepticism Descartes ended with the mind; Spinoza adhered to the will; Kant to categories; Hegel to structures; Kierkegaard to the leap of faith; Schopenhauer to the will; Nietzsche to the morality of victimhood; the French 20th century thinkers to the self.

CHAPTER ELEVEN - PHILOSOPHY PENETRATED, PART II

A: THE FIVE BRANCHES OF PHILOSOPHY

1 Ethics

Ethics starts in reality and then denies its origin. It searches for reality but then gives up and settles for expressions of the socio. The murderousness that everyone feels on some occasions (towards authority, parents, even children) gets smoothed into nice acceptable behaviour in order to preserve appearance. Yet ethics belongs in the area of 'is' rather than 'ought,' of excellence rather than of good versus bad; reality appears in it when ethics denotes worth rather than beliefs. Everyone is constantly trying to be good, so ethics has no need to become a utopian imposition of values geared to some kind of social engineering. When it does this it deviates from what people at the deepest level are trying to do. It becomes the over-cultivation of a natural process. The worst criminals in the world do not lack for goodness. But goodness gets lost or twisted because it is not thought through. It is distorted because of the input of others. The irony is that evil results from too much goodness. Lacking the capacity to think things through to the point of reality the criminal unthinkingly and excessively embraces an invocation to be good, and so ends by producing the opposite.

Problems arise because of a gap between intention and outcome. In the gap between the two lies an area of process where we can return to reality. The criminal's intention has been distorted because of the input of others so that the outcome is three or four moves away from his intention. The end result is unreality, death or suffering because outcome is so far removed from intention. Intention cannot know its outcome exactly beforehand. And if we focus solely on outcome we will be snatching at or forestalling the process that preceded it. The in-between area (reality) is difficult to relate to because it breeds uncertainty, and so is frequently replaced with intent or outcome or both. In other words, we foreclose reality. It is this area of process that has to be allowed to fructify and become the anchor for ethics. If there be an invocation at all it is to help the process and not fear it. Therapy says for example: feel everything more; go through the feelings and process them. Then there is no need to act them out. When the process is allowed to unfold we need no rules or authority to impose a predetermined code of behaviour. Life that is truly lived is always good. Evil is an accident waiting to happen because of ignorance of how to master the totality of things. Totality is not complex, but natural and rational. Reality finds its place in the lived life when we allow the chain reaction of events to unfold.

2 Logic

Logic is thinking that refuses to allow the possibility that resolution can arise between opposites. It has broken away from the incomparably grander concept of logos and hubristically claims to be equal to the whole. This inflated claim is the socio at work. Logos on the other hand allows us to see that non-opposing is pre-thinking. Pre-thinking is the state that prevailed before anxiety and intensity began to corrupt our thought processes, before we became persuaded that division was a natural way of thinking and state of being. Logos seeks to resolve the problems that logic has created. Logos has embraced all, from Aristotle onwards, by attempting to clarify the relation between opposites. Philosophy initiates a process of thinking which sweeps us along to ever more expansive conceptual frameworks. The obstacle to this movement is a perception of life as a problem. War, illness, mortality, morbidity – there are hundreds of ways of seeing life as a problem. And the origin of all these 'problems' can be found in the split thinking of logic.

Logic has been thought of as bullet-proof. But we can turn this contention on its head and ask:

why is logic seen as an answer to anything? Where Ayer sought answers there, Moore cautions us to see logic as 'arguably concerned with making sense of *sense*.'(1) Like mathematics, logic challenges many aspects of life, as in computing and IT. Yet when viewed philosophically it suffers from the hubristic claim to be the whole. What do we do with the 'fool-proof' claims of logic that things do not submit to resolution? Philosophy engages with myriad areas of life, like love, where logic cannot venture. Madness interacts with sanity rather than opposes it. Madness cannot be reduced to a single explanation – to the outcome of biology or environment – but must be connected to sanity or be dropped as a concept altogether.

Opposites are not mutually exclusive; indeed, aggregation offers a non-logical relationship between apparent opposites. An interaction amounting to a dynamic inclusivity that leads to creativity and interplay grows between apparently discrete entities. It doesn't matter whether or not one of the opposites rises as an inclusive category above the other (for good to include evil for instance) or another form of integration appears. All modes or entities interact curiously with each other: evil wants to explore good and ends up in a relationship to it that can lead to union, or to the evolution of a meta-concept within which both can find a home.

Philosophers can conceptualise any problem to the point where sharp distinctions are understood as impositions; it becomes clear that they arise ultimately from bad faith or a lack of authenticity. Thinking then impels us to diagnose the problem (by problematizing the problem) without falling onto one or other side of the divide. Ideas and issues are put into the melting pot and a solution emerges.

Logos gives us an opportunity to see that the logic of the future is an exploration of division. Philosophy engages with logic by asking questions about the philosophy of logic, not by asking about the logic of philosophy. Put another way, logic suffers from hubris, as do all branches of philosophy other than first philosophy, metaphysics. Though only a part, logic claims to configure the whole of philosophy. Logic is not a free-standing intellectual category above philosophy. Once we have found logic's proper place we have neutralised any need for a false conjunction. The question philosophy can now ask of logic is clear: what are its limits?

3 Aesthetics

Aesthetics has become a scientific discourse. Whereas Plato treats it as the idea of beauty (see below under Plato's three ontologies) aesthetics has become the study of form and representation of beauty. Beauty has been captured by subjectivity, as in phrases like 'beauty is in the eye of the beholder.' It even extends to a belief in the genius of the individual artist who produces inspiration *ab initio*. Yet the Greek myths understood the role of the muse to be that which connected a practitioner to a memory of reality. Connection is the key issue. This is shown in the example of the sculptor who chips away at his material to expose an image that is latent in the block of marble. The image was in effect drawn from the artist's memory of reality. Plato went further: he saw art as derivative (copying reality) and placed inspiration in the audience or the public. But whether it manifests in connection with the muse or the audience, connectivity lies at the heart of the aesthetic project. And this is the point of entry for contaminated thinking.

4 Epistemology

Epistemology begins with the notion of knowledge. To know is to be socialised. We cannot access ontology because of the tentacles of epistemology. This was the brunt of Socrates' attack. He turned our gaze from appearance and, by developing the idea of virtue, focused our gaze on ontology. The story goes that epistemology arose when people were told in ancient Egypt that there is something beyond mere use or application. The idea of knowledge then evolved into Plato's mind-reality dualism. The issue of how the mind knows eclipsed the issue of what there is to know. So strong is this preoccupation with the operation of mind that from Kant onwards epistemology has in effect included ontology! Why are we obsessed with epistemology? Because contaminated thinking latches on to the urge to know-perceive-grasp which dissociates us from the thing we seek to grasp. Philosophy is only concerned to know how we can grasp reality because reality already renders itself to be grasped. There is in fact no issue.

5 Political Philosophy

The ideas of a free citizenry, State, society, and governance early emerged as philosophical issues. However, even in Socrates' day, political philosophy was seen as a branch of ethics. This is because the idea of political philosophy is dualistic or oppositional: Hobbes dramatically pointed to naked self-interest in the relations between the individual and the State. This is the *ought* of ethics, rather than the *is* of philosophy.

Yet, the idea that a citizen *was* the State obtained from the beginning. The entry of dichotomies (citizen *vs* State) into this issue is not justified. When we recognise reality, governance is not a problem. Political philosophy has deteriorated from being the philosophy of the political into being a consensus of opinions in the political and public spheres. Socially-conformist thinking entered organised life at the outset; it is in the nature of tribes. Political philosophy has sustained this development by intruding ethics into communal life. This is unnecessary because individuals govern themselves as complex organisms; they have already integrated a governing system into this organism; only then do they reach out to spouse or friends. Political philosophy's attachment to the ought stops it raising its project to the level of philosophy. To do this it will have to stop imposing non-concepts, such as citizenship defined in opposition to State, on reality.

In any case, the State is a federal organisation containing cities and neighbourhoods. Both people and organisations are different in outlook but similar in process. Philosophy says there is no need to separate citizens and State. Political philosophy needs to be philosophised about. It is less a matter of what political philosophy says about the citizen than the questions philosophy asks of political philosophy, questions that have been asked from Plato to Rorty. The breaking away of political philosophy from philosophy itself has given the thinking of the zeitgeist a chance to become embedded. Because political philosophy is seen as rational in its own terms the power of social conformity in it has not been sufficiently explored. Politics has always been seen as 'the art of the possible,' a form of thinking that has escaped philosophical scrutiny and has allowed social conformity to flourish.

B: THE FOUR EXPLANATORY SYSTEMS OF PHILOSOPHY

Explanatory systems seek to grant us freedom by giving us knowledge of our thinking processes and of the formation of our material or social world. But the interplay between the causes in the explanatory schemes has led to a belief in agency. Teleology persuades us that we are moving towards the Good of Plato or along a path of causation towards the intelligible world of Aristotle. The idea of perfectibility or intelligibility holds everything together irrespective of the diversity of the separate factors. There is general agreement that there are four ways to explain everything from the meaning of truth to the nature of Being. For instance Aristotle's materialism seeks to explain how a thing comes to be: the material (matter out of which the thing is made); the actually existing being necessary to initiate and sometimes carry through the process of coming into being of a material thing, the form of the thing which gives it its definite being; and the final cause, end or purpose for which the thing comes into being. Schopenhauer's four explanations are: causal, logical, mathematical, and action. Badiou focuses on truth-procedures in the areas of love, politics, science and art. Yet whichever way knowledge is dissected in an attempt to identify the key areas of the lived life or the methods that access reality, the feature that stands out is that all four explanations have to relate to each other. Interconnection is the chief message irrespective of which factors are identified. Social conformity is very clever – it is not the thing-in-itself but it is that which binds or connects anything to anything else.

C: THE THREE EPISTEMOLOGIES: SCIENCE, ART AND RELIGION

The claims of science, the philosophical concept of beauty and the religious concept of God are all corrupted. They are ways of looking at reality rather than of operating within it. They see the universal only in the unique which then accentuates the place of self. Searching not for reality but for states of mind, they ask only how we know anything. All three epistemologies offer to train the mind in order to *see* something; yet what they see is already decided by peer-agreement. Science exists, so Heidegger observed, to 'amass and clarify bits of knowledge,' and even then 'no amount of scientific rigour attains to the seriousness of metaphysics.'(2) Infinity is an act of faith in science because it cannot survey all cases without limit. In the case of art, the mind is expanded in an attempt to get it to correspond to reality; but it only fits into the space established by our existing social territory. It has expanded overall only temporarily until a regression to the norm or to 'human nature' ensues. Hollywood scriptwriters cleverly use a warping effect when they present a socialised view of beauty. Indeed, art in general becomes a reflection of social values when it gives a spurious unity to things that then projects a dangerous correspondence between audience and scriptwriter, playwright or author. In this respect art's popularising use of beauty is similar to the role of the congregation in religions. The congregation emerges as the centrepiece of religion (God fading into the background) because the congregation is a nexus of agreed views on scripture. In science, art and religion discourse converges on the mean as it accommodates to socially-amenable topics of discussion. In contrast, as Wittgenstein tells us, philosophy leaves everything as it is.

D: PLATO'S THREE ONTOLOGIES

The more virtuous we become the more real we are: this is the message of Socrates and Plato. It is not about being right. The Greek word arête translates as excellence, aptitude, to be grounded, to be true to one's nature. All the virtues were for Plato different ways of looking at the same thing: a single life governed by reason. As such, the three virtues of goodness, truth and beauty are invitations to reality: we become more real as we gain self-knowledge. The virtues are not projections of the human mind; they are not desires or objectives. They are already in reality waiting to be uncovered, like a sculptor reveals the form inside a block of marble. Virtue is a springboard from which to take things further in wonderment rather than to ossify around a given level of understanding. It is not a pre-emptive leap to conclusions or actions. To get near to the true meaning of virtue usually involves the reversal of modern interpretations of it. In this way the modern predilection for development or outcome can be circumvented and virtue returned to its original meaning of function, aptitude, or of being true to its purpose. Virtue is concerned with what draws it forward (telos) to a given function and in the process reveals its true nature. For example modern child development says that children are innocent of moral failings but that the adult is judgemental and accountable. But, following Socrates, we can say that if an adult led a life true to his own nature then he would become even more good, true and beautiful than is an innocent child.

Socrates took the issue of virtue further by combining each with reason. Nietzsche was wrong to accuse Socrates of relying heavily on reason. Neither virtue nor reason alone helps us to traverse the realm between us and the absolute. Together they create an enhancement of both. For example, the Platonic Good combines all splits, whereas good in an ordinary sense means only the opposite of bad, a topic for social argumentation. Method is the genesis of the harmony of all things.

Problems arise when virtues are taken from the metaphysical realm and placed in the existential world of appearances, dichotomies, judgements and action. Because of this wrenching move each virtue has suffered a debasement since Plato. Goodness has become identified with ethics; truth has become fragmented; and beauty associated primarily with what Plato called simulacra, copies of the real, or with erotic expressions of love. As an entry to this topic however I will for the moment deem the three virtues to be reality.

i) GOODNESS

Socrates was the champion of the good, but he did so with his famed irony. Even Plato approaches it in this spirit. Kierkegaard wrote his thesis on Socratic irony. The problem is that knowledge of it is taken to lie deep inside and it needs to be teased out. The ontological status of the good is confusing because it is expressed in the language of philosophical provocation. Yet Socrates found his life mission as a questioner who teased out of friends in the Agora an appreciation of the good that lay deep inside them.

The notion of goodness reached its zenith during the Greek Golden Age. It is arguably at the core of the Platonic oeuvre. It encompassed more than it does nowadays, as the long-drawn-out change in the meaning of goodness from kindness to utility illustrates. This is also seen in the shift from excellence to rightness and from clarity to congruence. In other words, goodness held all virtues accountable to itself and was indispensable to harmony during the Greek Golden Age. It was synonymous with unity, approximated to nature, and came near to embodying reason and moderation. In short, it underpinned life and the universe. It might even be said to have held in suspension beauty (Plato's nemesis) and truth (Plato's Sphinx:

stubborn and undecipherable). Goodness invites us to think in the most penetrating way about reality. Before Socrates, reality was recognised as the elements of water, fire, air and earth. The concepts of nous and logos were just beginning to appear. So goodness appeared at the heart of reality by in effect taking the place of the elements. Nonetheless goodness is not real; late in Plato's life he believed that Socrates' mission to reach virtue was unachievable in the everyday sense of 'doing good.' In other words, there is no goodness as we search for it; it is already there in ways we have yet to discover; it is thrown up into the world occasionally only to be discarded. We need not read too much into this concept. But Plato was such a great mind that he couldn't fail to see the metaphysical import of goodness. He makes clear that we become more real when we understand this idea. Conversely we entrench the doctrinal or ideological claims of the zeitgeist when, without understanding the idea, we seek to 'do good'.

The Socratic sense of goodness is completeness, connecting up all the dots, going through the manifest to the intent that lies deeper. Conversely, ethics deals in good *versus* bad (splits, opposites) and says for example that only the innocent or non-criminal is good. Socrates saw that what ethics defines as bad is an expression of that which is lacking or not acknowledged in what ethics defines as good. For example, Socrates' view encompasses the idea that the criminal has good intentions, indeed that he might have been seeking to be *too* good. This view allows for evil to be an excess of good that is only described as evil because it frightens others into shying away from it. As a result it is expelled to another realm. Contemporary thinking - from the message in Golding's *Lord of the Flies* to views about insanity and claims that things are more real in a battle – says that reality produces evil. Rather, I argue, when people become frightened their thinking becomes oppositional. Evil is then seen as an ethical category. Nonetheless, evil is still within reality. In other words, to think of evil is to think fearfully.

The world does not lack for goodness; the problem is that we do not understand the idea. Socrates accepted that we may never acquire a comprehensive understanding of it, but he makes clear that seeking to act without lengthy open-minded pondering is the problem the world faces. Plato saw no purpose in pursuing knowledge and reason per se; he only did so because they facilitated the search for goodness.

How then do we move from the modern sense of ethical 'doing good' to an understanding of goodness? It is ironic that everyone seems already to know goodness or to have values that underpin their actions – to care for young children and old people and so on – and would claim that their action is far from being unexamined or a response to sentiment or appearance! Ethics is an enquiry into how to do good without understanding the idea.

It is usual to say that goodness is a self-evident virtue. But Plato reveals it to be the least obvious and most provocative of Greek virtues. It is moderately easy to understand aesthetics or metaphysics for instance. But the endless ethical arguments over goodness have made it the least accessible of concepts. For example, it might seem ethically obvious to give to charity, and yet charity might cause the problem it claims to alleviate. We need to take goodness out of the realm of ethics, where it stands in opposition to bad, creating a gap for social conformity to enter. Goodness can then be said to possess the highest ontological status. Yet this claim only becomes clear if we are prepared to travel to the heart of reality to find it.

ii) TRUTH

Truth has been seen as synonymous with reality. Marx famously described truth as 'knowing reality.' We may ask how we can know it, but truth is not an issue of how we know. There is no doubt: reality just is. Social thinking takes over when we insist on knowing how we know. To doubt is to question whether we can know truth, not to doubt that it is. The observer is there to observe that which is, but truth is in the area of ontology, not epistemology. Truth is within is-ness or reality; as such it is related to many other areas such as goodness. It is totality; it confounds all attempts to clarify it by splitting it (into right and wrong for instance). We are attracted to it as an idea or Form, whether we like it or not. We are accountable to truth, seek to reach it and, in the attempt, we find it works its way into life, whether we seek it or not.

Totality is so much more than the aspects of it that our thoughts solidify around. Truth encompasses all the attempts we make to reach reality, and all opposites. Liars are truth-tellers (attempting a truth). Deceit is only the unravelling of something we don't yet know.

Theories of truth become bogged down in aspects of knowledge such as doubt, falsification and so on. There is perhaps no idea that has become more fragmented, misused, corrupted, perverted and desecrated than truth. In the light of sustained attacks on truth from philosophers over the past 100 years or so we may feel that we have reached a point where it has run its course and needs to be abandoned. Alternatively, we may see our current confusions over the idea as a call to try and understand it better.

Socrates offered an alternative to the usual sense of knowledge when he said he knew that he did not know. There is no knowledge he can know, but he still knows. So, we can start by seeing truth as something that is at one with its object; something that achieves peace and harmony between all inner aspects of an entity. This is another way of expressing the concept of the thing-in-itself, an entity or idea that is true to its own nature or function. This concept reconciles Parmenides' idea of oneness with Heraclitus' idea of change: truth is the capacity to see one side of a divide as the unexamined aspects of its counterpart.

The task of truth is to bring mind and reality into relationship. Until we know truth we cannot reach out to what it resides in - reality. It is a commitment on the behalf of the philosopher to get as close as possible to reality. Mind takes us away from ourselves; philosophy is a return to our true self. In a sense we are mind-penetrated, open to our own doubts, not real. Truth offers us a commitment that the object is more real than the subject. So, where Freud says the ego (mind) replaces the id (nature, object), we say the id is visceral human reality. Descartes made clear that we can use the mind to subject itself to an exploration of what ontologically underpins the mind. In this way the commitment of truth is to a fuller integration of mind into reality.

iii) BEAUTY

Beauty is said to be in the eye of the beholder, which means it is easy to confuse physical beauty with the abstract concept of beauty. Plato tells us beauty grows as we experience and understand erotic love, when we as subjects apprehend (fall into or are taken by) the external world through our senses. It is only at the outset, in the form of erotic love, that beauty is concerned with the physical. The famous Diotima passage in Plato's *Symposium* explains how passion or erotic love takes us first into the thickets of personal existence and then, so long as one contemplates the process as it unravels, universalises experience until it transforms into an appreciation of the essence (or as Plato has it, the soul) of the object of love, and finally takes us to the very *idea* of beauty. At this point harmony appears, things connect, the real emanates. In other words, beauty bridges the perceived split between two selves - body and mind - and between existence and essence. In George Santayana's words (which pick up the themes in the Diotima passage), 'The passions, in so far as they are impulses to action, entangle us materially in the flux of substance, being intent on seizing, transforming, or destroying something that exists; but at the same time, in so far as they quicken the mind, they are favourable to the discernment of essence; and it is only a passionate soul that can be truly contemplative. The reward of the lover, which also chastens him, is to discover that, in thinking he loved anything in this world, he was profoundly mistaken. Everybody strives for possession; that is the animal instinct on which everything hangs; but possession leaves the true lover unsatisfied: his joy is in the character of the thing loved, in the essence it reveals, whether it be here or there, now or then, his or another's. This essence, which for action was only a signal letting loose a generic animal impulse, to contemplation is the whole object of love, and the sole gain in loving.' (3)

Thus reality can be reached by singularity as well as inclusivity. Some things are perceived to be so intense or overriding that they cannot be resisted. It is a challenge to accept that some things dare to be without at least offering some justification; that they claim their virtue by distinction from others or reality at large.

The aesthetic is about exceptionalism. It recognises that Helen of Troy's unique beauty meant that all beauty must thereafter be copies of the singular original. Exceptionalism goes against the grain of other aspects of philosophy which stress integration. But every entity can be exceptional; exceptionalism doesn't preclude integration; reality after all is everything. The idea that things stand apart allows us to play with reality. To foreground something or grant it selective importance vis a vis other things (though not at their expense) is the act of a Greek god (or a camera). This is not to create a hierarchy - selective importance might be withdrawn, needless to say! Playing on the idea of difference is another royal road to reality.

SUMMARY

All the founding ideas in philosophy, with the exceptions of metaphysics, philosophical method and the body, are parts of reality making claims to be the whole. On the one hand, philosophy asks us to let go of looking in order to see things. Yet, on the other hand, philosophy's founding ideas are concerned with ways of looking at things in order to know them (epistemology) or to subject them to peer-agreement. They are constrained by their partiality and by the nature of the questions they ask, which are from the point of view of mind rather than reality. Even Plato's ontologies struggle to be both universal and particular at the same time.

Yet it needs saying that every aspect of reality is a thing-in-itself that can be subjected to scrutiny and brought under the injunction to 'know thyself.' For example, each of the ontologies appears to approach reality differently. Goodness is harmony and the joining-up-of-the-dots; truth takes us to the object; beauty sees the universe in the utterly singular, exceptional grain of sand. When fully expressed they converge on each other in reality. Plato was wary of beauty, and his search for truth was so difficult that he was left only with goodness. His greatest contribution was to tell us that a virtue is a metaphysical concept, a given or *a priori* that cannot be 'applied' in the world until its metaphysical import is understood. Action is not the object; action without understanding arises from fear; it makes understanding even more difficult to achieve. It allows social pressures to undermine virtue

SECTION FIVE: (RE)DISCOVERING REALITY

CHAPTER TWELVE - PHILOSOPHY RESURGENT: METAPHYSICS

I start this chapter with Franz Rosenzweig's claim that an agitated mind risks destroying human connection. Agitated minds, he explains, do this because they cherish the world, set out to woo it and eventually to master it. In contrast, he contends, calm, open-ended thinking remains attentive to whatever presents itself. It recognises the integrity of what is presented, merely observing it rather than seeking to comprehend it fully. I take it that it is calm thinking's lack of possessiveness that allows thinking to take us to the universal and to stay there. And only in this way can thinking unrelentingly engage with the nature of things. Metaphysics might be conceived of in this way. When we accept that universality is attained by collapsing the known into the unknown we can see why it takes calm thinking to go beyond the known into the unknown. Calm and boundless thinking works to combat the confusion to which we are prone when we try to make sense of things. As Moore puts it, 'Metaphysics should and can help us make sense of ourselves.' (1) It is directly related to suffering because, without a foundation in reality (boundlessness), our thinking will bifurcate and create anxiety and alienation. Our relation to others becomes unclear. Yet, used simply, the mind can correct its own distortions and allow thinking to connect to reality.

The Greeks didn't try to understand reality; they lived it with open minds. When Plato wrote of 'return' he meant not only that a man or woman could act as if a god, but that thinking could become metaphysical again. The time has come to return metaphysics to its place as first philosophy, in the clear conviction that, as Moore expresses it: 'To whatever extent the unexamined life is not worth living, neither is the life without metaphysics.' (2) Philosophy is a last hope, like the Dutch boy with his finger in the dyke. It is not difficult to envisage a world devoid of metaphysics as a world devoid of reality! The test of any proposition is always how well it sits with reality. It becomes a matter of how we use our minds: do we accept what mind tells us in its uncultivated, socially-infected state or do we cultivate it? Only in the latter case will we clear away what obstructs our view of the big picture. Philosophy is wholly about the big picture. It starts with a claim that reality is *a priori* to any claim I might make on the basis of a 'personal' mind. From this it follows that philosophy is also *a priori* to any claim to prioritise any one branch of it. The point has been emphasised on earlier pages that when we attempt to elevate or separate any one branch of philosophy we are conferring ontological status on mind-constructs and letting the bifurcating tendency of mind go unquestioned. This and the following two chapters will discuss the *a priori* status of reality. But, for the moment and in brief, my reasoning goes like this: because I can think to the universal or think abstractly it follows that the concepts I am thinking are already there waiting to be thought. The connection between thinking and reality is there at the outset and only awaits recognition. 'I' do not think or 'create' the universe; 'I' am a manifestation of the universe which itself possesses a reflective capacity. Thus, the universe thinks through me. In that sense 'I' am in effect an eddy in the bend of a river. The river continues to flow through me even though an observer might claim to perceive a movement that distinguishes itself from the rest of the river.

Metaphysics looks for the meta-concepts that bridge dichotomies; in so doing it reveals the underlying harmony of the universe. Plato thought of it as the desire for what is beyond my immediate reality. Metaphysics locates underlying harmony by seeing the observer as reality self-observing. This does not close down or reject any manifestation of reality; rather, it adds to internal multiplicity and complexity and embraces all dualisms. The failure to reveal this harmony leaves us with a world prone to dichotomous thinking. This is what happens when we abandon metaphysics. What is wanted, as the age-old body-mind conundrum is telling us, is how to understand that thinking and living are one and the same. It involves accepting the complexity of reality without having a need to force resolution onto it in the form of a dichotomy. Spinoza told us that recognition of the universe as *a priori* is *the* single condition that has to be met if we are to sustain human wellbeing. All kind of questions may then be asked about the place of welfare states, national health services, ethics, morality and politics in a world open to greater reality. These questions will be addressed in Chapter Fifteen.

To be alive is to encounter reality daily. Someone argues with me or I knock against a table and I am alert to something I wasn't a moment before. In both these cases the senses are my connection to the world. I see, smell, hear or touch something and my thinking sets out to apprehend what my senses engage with. In other words, thought arises in response to my being in the world, a world that is there before my senses engage with it. When I think I respond to the call of reality.

Explanations of this move abound: the Neo-Platonists, Spinoza, Nietzsche, Heidegger and

Deleuze have argued the case for immanence, for a joining up of the dots in the universe, so to speak. The matter hinges on the nature and quality of thinking. Entities can make a clean contact with each other only when dualist concepts like difference are show to be a device that can be extended to infinity. For instance, unity embraces multiplicity and plurality. Spinoza, Nietzsche and Deleuze challenged a prevailing fixation with subjectivity, and directed attention to the nature of immanence and flux. Moreover, Spinoza leans towards locating thinking in the body. When thinking is harmonious, that is, when it is anchored, it operates in the purely functional or reflective mode; when it becomes intense, agitated or reflexive it has lost its anchor and starts to become a law unto itself

The key word is thinking. Yet it must first be made clear that mind is not thought; rather, mind is itself a concept that thinking has conceived in order to act as a holder of thought. As a framework imposed on thought mind actually impedes the free flow of thought; its attempt to structure thought means it constantly veers towards a position or a resting-place. The holding or defending of a position is a reactive process that denies the effervescence of thought. A philosophical conversation is a never-ending process whereby reality is expressed through an idea that at some time gives rise to a position. With felicitous exchange this position will eventually rise to a meta-position. This process allows positions to open to possibilities and thus release thinking to engage with the next set of sense-perceptions without prejudgement. Philosophy begins in the wonder of the unanalysed moment. Wonderment is not a form of heightened or enhanced experience. It is the sense of immediacy to or congruence with what is happening. Nothing is added, but nothing is avoided or obscured.

We rely on metaphysics to prevent the relationship between mind and reality from tilting too far towards mind. Mind, it is worth remembering, is a concept that attempts to understand thinking. As such, it is a second move; it cannot leap ahead of reality or create it in totality. If mind is a second move then so is subjectivity. For mind, as Foucault reminds us, has been treated as the mind of men or women. Individuation, desire and drive – the meat of psychology – have in recent thinking replaced metaphysics as a guide to a fully lived life. Indeed psychological ideas have taken deep root in contemporary philosophy. Yet, there is something patriarchal about the way mind moves towards a dominance of reality. It might be surmised that metaphysics is in some sense a feminine counterbalance. Philosophy, it must forever be emphasised, is not philosophy of mind but rather of the relationship that develops between mind and reality. Philosophy gains its energy and rationale from this exercise. By maintaining thinking at the universal, metaphysics not only enables is-ness to obtain, it also opens the door to potential.

CHAPTER THIRTEEN - PHILOSOPHY RESURGENT: METHOD

GENERAL

Despite the frailties of philosophy indicated in earlier chapters philosophical method has never been intrinsically unfit for purpose. It has enabled us to see that the old questions concerning ontology, epistemology and ethics are no longer pressing concerns. The challenge for method is now the socio. Philosophy's ignorance of this force hitherto attests to philosophy's failure to meet any deep needs. Concepts such as mind, will and justice were once seen as subversive but now appear as secondary issues at best. The human condition is tragic because the socio enters our existence at the very point where we seek to remove obstacles to our wellbeing. It attaches itself to our search for liberty, goodness, the divine, and the rational. People work hard to achieve self-awareness, only for the socio to thrive on the search for spirituality, work, meaning, and transcendence. No wonder people finally become cynical and turn away defeated.

New philosophical questions have to be asked, the foremost of which is clearly: why do people embrace the socio even at their own expense? The alternatives to philosophy are unable to answer this question. Morality is based on dichotomous thinking that drives thought along channels that diverge from reality. Artistic expression doesn't make clear what is being expressed or what the relation of that is to reality. Religion believes in an authority outside the universe and so denies the potential of the human mind (however contorted its common usage) to apprehend the world. To give a free-standing status to a fragment of reality, in the way of science, is to give meaning to a particularity without reference to the whole. To believe the universe can be comprehended without fully engaging with thought, as does mysticism, is to deny the capacity of thinking to access reality. All these problems arise because of the contradictory uses to which we put mind. It is the only faculty we have to clear the clutter that gets in our way; yet mind is only a part of reality; its vantage point is partial and changeable. It is not surprising that classical philosophy treated appearance, opinions and feelings about reality with profound scepticism. Nor is it surprising that the questioning of claims rather than the making of them was for Socrates the basis of philosophical enquiry.

The notion of philosophy runs as a thread through all attempts at philosophising. It is as if one is part of a grand thought-experiment or an ongoing working hypothesis. In this space thinking takes a break from the relentless notion of life, from our habits and habituations, from a self-imposed pressure for justification, prioritisation, purposefulness, functionality, and its dependence on an accustomed, unexamined benchmark to measure itself against. Here, philosophy itself is the benchmark, holding in suspense for all eternity that which, by the very idea of philosophy, depends on it. Namely, everything is still open, up for grabs, otherwise possible, yet-to-come, within the realm of consideration. And, until philosophy has thought everything through (admittedly a long-range project), what we do or don't do really doesn't matter; everything can pass as arbitrary, can be swapped, shifted and changed, merely accentuating its false and dichotomised nature.

Philosophy invites us to consider adversity as intimacy. Any attempt to explore a relation between mind and reality already counts itself as part of the project even if it constitutes a wedge between them. The cardinal point is that philosophy invites us to go beyond our cosy constructs (or simulacra), be it postmodernist, Kantian, or otherwise. The *a priori* - that which we don't (yet) think - is the very foundation of our thought, a step from nothing-ness to something-ness (and vice versa) compelling upon us (if we allow) a notion above categories and beyond classifications - not what we think but that we think.

Philosophy asks great questions from an Archimedean standpoint, outside or above all things. Everything is open to rational explanation; nothing lies outside the pale. Philosophy is thus a fulcrum that uses leverage to move the very Earth itself. (1) Parmenides, Zeno and the Eleatic School believed truth could only be attained by their method of arguing from sound premises; they disdained sense experience. Socrates was sure that the way he went about things (his method) was more important than the content or outcome of his method. Wittgenstein concurred, claiming that philosophy is an activity (qua method). Thus, philosophical method reveals itself simply as a relationship, a way of bridging splits and polarities. The method is thus a conversation between positions, an embrace of all from a meta-position, shifting and adjusting in order to examine and accommodate new positions. The birth of new concepts arises within the interrelationship of old ones, themselves often strange bedfellows. No juxtaposition is rejected. Much of the time everything in life might appear to be random and arbitrary. Philosophy makes clear that what seems random has in fact been selectively drawn from the whole, while claiming to stand in for it. When we subscribe to a belief in randomness we prevent totality emerging. Totality allows that which was not selected to stand alongside that which was. Most life endeavours succumb to this fragmentation and selectivity. Inertia is the result. Philosophy exposes the arbitrariness of these selections.

Philosophy in the person of Plato (and thinkers of the Axial Age) opened up a gap between mind and body that Spinoza partially closed. We cannot now turn away from monism. The opening of this gap offered opportunities for further thought - such as the development of speculative philosophy and a focus on the tension between Being and the lived life. But this gap is itself the socio. We don't need it; indeed it is a puzzle why Spinoza's work was not able to put a stop to the obsession with it. The long years of fascination with epistemology can only be explained as a failure to heed Spinoza.

The usual description of philosophy is: thinking about thinking. We test our ordinary thinking about things (as they appear to us) against reality. To philosophise is to stop thinking exclusively in terms of ourselves. By moving away from self-centredness we can keep our eye on the absolute, which is of course everything there is. Then we can use it as an anchor when opinions and attitudes threaten to drive our thinking along fixed channels. We often find that the level of our daily thinking fails us; we realise we have stepped away from reality into a world of opinions and attitudes because we want to hold on to certainty in our daily life. Yet, the more we recognise the existence of a gap the more we grow. Scepticism makes us realise how questionable is our daily thinking; it can do this because from the outset it accepts the existence of the absolute. Socrates suggested we connect with reality when we cast doubt on human institutions. He loved people but saw all around him people abandoning the absolute, even when they turned to God as an institutionalisation of the absolute. There are many false absolutes with the power to side-track us - nature, reason and knowledge for instance - which are merely particularities within the absolute.

Philosophy seeks to connect us to everything there is (the world of positions included) without limitations such as duration, category or the inherent limitations found in any particular way of thinking. It is concerned with flow or process, with raising thought to ever-higher levels that can challenge what we subjectively claim to experience. It is not concerned with positions, outcomes, conclusions or meanings. It sees no virtue in a discussion ossifying around a position, however profound its implication or how much thought has been put into getting to that position or indeed whether it promises a glimpse of knowledge, truth or God. Positions are a product of the daily world we inhabit, the world of structures, finitude, narratives and contingency. To hold a position is to be held in aspic by structures of thought that emanate from logic, circumstance and zeitgeist. Philosophy challenges meaning, which is sharply defined in order for people to feel certain and operate in the world. Reality by contrast is undefined. Philosophy is not a practice in the sense that religions (or spiritual movements like Buddhism) are. It doesn't set out to offer wise words or spiritual guidance. That is not the wisdom that the Greeks are said to have loved.

Constant questioning allows process to flow. As conclusions arise they are questioned, and then questioned again. So relentless is the questioning process and so little status is accorded the answers or positions that occasionally arise that questioning itself is seen as the fulcrum on which all else hinges. Because any outcome or position is a product of mind that claims premature validity the questioning method itself emerges as the only thing that connects us to reality. It is sometimes called the fulcrum method. With reference to the absolute it is the philosophical thing-in-itself. The machinations of the mind are stilled and the perceived gap between subject and object closes.

Aporia is a Greek word that describes the moment when the internal contradictions and rigidities of mind collapse and thereby reveal what an otherwise overactive or rigid mind conceals. The deceptive web begins to break down; particularisation loses its power to create structures, interpretations, explanations, beginnings and endings, plans and scenarios.

To say that 'reality is everything' is a mind-construct that is easily understood. Yet, as was discussed in Chapter Two, the phrase 'reality is everything there is' opens this phrase to greater reality the longer we ponder and question it. It cannot be pinned down, defined or explained. It is a conundrum that constantly provokes the mind to go beyond established constructs, eventually even to leave constructs behind. It provokes us to experiment with the operation of logic, not to reject it but to try more intuitive methods or ones that stretch or play with logic.

In this sense philosophy lies in the gap between 'everything' and 'everything there is.' It is not an intellectual exercise (in the sense connoted by theories of mind) but a method of checking out the operation of the mind *as a part of reality*. It does this by universalising everything the mind produces so that the mind cannot settle on a position. When a position begins to emerge it is questioned relentlessly. It becomes clear that the phrase 'reality is everything' must have emerged from a world that is committed to a belief in purpose, narrative, logic and certainty-seeking. Socrates upset this uneasily-cosy and fear-ridden world for ever when he said that what is good is not good because it is right but because it is true. In other words, good does not conform to attempts to structure it but it responds to attempts to free it.

A way to understand the claims made about reality by the faculty of mind (and by mental tools such as reason and knowledge) is to conduct a thought-experiment. First we hold reality constant. Then the 'realities' that mind, reason and knowledge offer us reveal their partiality. They are seen now as separate from the totality of reality, however elusive that concept is. Moreover, we can more clearly see the assumptions we make as we claim to 'know' or 'experience' reality. The way the faculty of mind has fragmented reality becomes apparent. All great thinkers start to philosophise about reality by isolating the refracting lenses through which we perceive or construe it. And then they have one big idea that they cannot resist presenting; their thinking ossifies around that idea. Eventually someone will appear who is less concerned to take a position and the process begins again.

We may never 'know' or explain reality yet the search for it remains the Holy Grail and sets the bar high for all of philosophy. We are here concerned with the foundational question of philosophy (sometimes called first philosophy) - what is a thing? (2) Also known as 'fulcrum reality,' it is impersonal, abstract, purist metaphysics. The idea of reality implies that the mind and so much else is superfluous or, as Spinoza would say, but a property, attribute or mode. A monist explanation or model of reality holds all human endeavours in suspension for the duration in pursuit of the 'divine,' which lies neither in the heavens nor on earth, but at the heart of all there is. Because reality is a given, any attempt to step over it by consciousness only leads to confusion. The more we think the more we overshoot. But reality is there and so we miss it.

So, for now, philosophy is a work-in-progress, a 'passing of the thread' endeavour within which literally anything goes, so long as it is committed to the philosophical project. It might be taken for granted that all positions embrace the idea of philosophy, and it is only in the name of it, on its behalf as it were, recognising and reconnoitring other positions (already stated and yet to come, in agreement or opposed) that the work of philosophy, its very being, comes to be. For, what else is philosophy if not an exploratory, investigative, reaching out, forever-considering enterprise? How can a position come to be if not aware of its inverse as twin, mirror-image, negation or affirmation? In all these senses it is fair to say that holding a position is anti-philosophical. On the other hand, to understand the emergence, the love-hate relationship, the interplay and the pregnant tension involved between positions is to notice the mind becoming aware that others think otherwise, that it is possible to think otherwise, that that which we negate or oppose is nonetheless valid and holds claim to the same ideals to which we hold. We realise we are travellers on the same journey, sharing destination, method, love, commitment, self-discipline, and as such unite in a meta-position. Heraclitus' formula was unity-in-multiplicity, at once recognising difference and integration.

METHOD

There is no method *in* philosophy; philosophy *is* method. Until we take categories from the usual definition of method we will not think. The crux of philosophy is never to abandon the absolute. So we can say at the outset that reality anchors method as an idea. Method is not susceptible to an organising principle. It annihilates the category by which we try to organise it. This forces us to go back and look at categories again. It could result in us abandoning categorisation altogether. For the moment this may be too big a step. Yet, method takes us on the journey, and that may be all that matters.

Method is philosophy's way of using mind to free us from the effects of its own mischief. To this end philosophy is nothing but method, a thread that has often been hidden from sight, but has nonetheless persisted tenaciously throughout the history of philosophy, irrespective of the changing preoccupations of its branches. Method releases us into spontaneity and authenticity, to total freedom from all constraints. It helps us to let go of knowledge and to open to process by using questions to liberate the questioned from their own minds. Only then, as Heidegger put it, can we begin to think. The process of questioning has become the thing-in-itself because, however profound the ideas we put in place of others, they are still only a higher class of clutter, when we ultimately want our minds emptied. Questioning releases all entities from the ties of definition, association or identification. For example, a journey is usually seen as leading to a destination. Yet, philosophical method says a journey is a journey in its own right. This seems outrageously counter-intuitive; it is clearly a threat to propositional thinking. Yet it is based on the idea that only truly-free entities can enter into relationship with other truly-free entities. Without method we would subsist on a contaminated version of freedom, one that depends on partial truths that circumscribe and qualify reality. Because the methods used by all academic disciplines are geared to a partial view of reality (because they are all sub-divisions of philosophy) we possess only philosophical method with which to sweep aside all the rubble that keeps us in a zombie state.

Method starts with a hypothesis, as is the case in any area of enquiry; but it then asks: what is outside our thinking? Method is a challenge to thinking itself. This is Nietzsche's point – all philosophers have sacrificed method in the end and settled for an outcome that is practical and comprehendible. Kant separated reason from everything else for example. The result is that the tensions within reality have been ignored or down-played. The tension is between the part and the whole. The betrayer of reality is the part. As has sometimes been said of Christianity, the disciples betrayed Jesus by differing. The onus is on us from the very start to kill all the gods that lead us to separation, and to ignore our tendency to particularise and split. Philosophy challenges the view that the world rests on a seemingly obvious notion of clear-cut, well-defined boundaries. Thus, a toy is a toy; a tree is just a tree; and anything under the sun (including the sun itself, of course) is evidently itself. But is this really the case? As we all eventually find out, appearances can be deceptive, naïve conceptions unravel as constructs, and categories may well emerge as but manifestations of the very process of categorisation itself. For example, scientific advances unfold fundamentals of particle/wave fluctuations, a field of forces and interactions binding entities together, a subjective gaze capable of determining the very reality of an object observed, and a variation within entities exceeding the difference between them. Are we not, the question must be asked, using short-cuts and opting for convenience when we refer to reality as an aggregate of distinct things? We need to discuss the pros and cons of an approach where stubbornly-held notions of fixed-boundary, ring-fenced entities are persistently and enthusiastically prioritised over dynamic relationships. Are we not talking about reality-in-the-making where things, entities, and selves are but a representational mask covering what happens when we encounter each other?

So, philosophical method is the stripping away of all external criteria and validations. The idea of truth can never be enhanced by measuring its effect against an inevitable bias towards the familiar, comfortable and conventional. We get to the truth by giving it the respect it deserves as an idea waiting to be born, perhaps already existing in embryo. It encompasses its own totality, bursting into our consciousness as a journey unto itself. What then is a journey if it is not a destination nor yet a journey? The mind plays tricks, offering proximate targets in its tendency to break down the journey into mini non-journeys, thereby never truly leaving home. We can take it then that we rarely if ever undertake a real journey. Hence the invitation to embark on method in order to start a journey; otherwise we are destined to solidify and repeat, locked within perplexity and responding to whim, forever pursuing ends without undertaking a beginning.

Thus method is a fulcrum that reveals all from under the aspect of eternity. Philosophy is not anthropomorphic; it operates in the area that lies between us and the absolute. There are of course no entities in the universe (absolute). But, when traversing the area between us and the absolute, philosophy has been forced traditionally to move along two axes. The first involves seeing reality as totality. There is nothing in reality that doesn't exist as a concept. Reality has no properties: it isn't an entity and cannot be right or wrong. It embraces all that is not yet conceived as well as all that has already been conceived, all that has not yet lived as well as all that is living, and so on. It may be said that Plato's emphasis on ideas has made the totality axis seem remote and alienating compared to the second axis, which is reality as existence. This axis sees reality in terms of the lived life, of experience, knowledge and so on. Philosophy constantly unites the two strands when they begin to pull apart. Conceptualisation does this for example when it denies non-existence from claiming separate status by including it within existence itself. As a result harmony prevails.

THE CONCEPT

At the heart of the philosophical quest is the concept. A concept is greater than the object on which it focuses. When we first see an object we only attain a kind of non-comprehension, which sets in train a process of reducing it to manageable proportions so that we can docket or identify it. (3) When we conceptualise an object we see it in its full glory, more than the object itself can manifest, so to speak. Under intense scrutiny ideas about reality will collapse as an earlier failure to reason becomes apparent. At some point even great ideas reveal splits or lacunae. For example Marxism sought happiness at the expense of the individual. In any case a concept is only the presently-accepted reality. If the concept appears immoveable its connection to reality is revealed as a retreat or second move. Discussion of the concept has the power to close the gap between the concept and the object to which it pertains. This is why Plato is wrongly described as a dualist; he sought to bridge concept and object.

Yet_Plato's metaphysics_eventually_led_us_into a blind_alley. We_are_in_his_debt_for_tackling_the emergence of mind. But, as a result, he privileged mind over reality, the very source from which it had emerged. We can retrace his steps to the point where he expressed reality in the concept. This intellectual method allows us to avoid thinking that the product of mind is reality itself. Nonetheless, a concept is only a means to an end. Ultimately, we can posit, philosophy will kill all concepts in a Masada-like finale, the last two concepts cancelling each other out. Of course the sheer amount of philosophical work needed before we can reach this point is huge. We must address Plato's Forms and then let them go; then address logic and then let it go; address God then let Him go, and finally concepts themselves and let them go. At this point we will have let go of everything, have emptied ourselves of mind and opened ourselves up for reality to enter. While this is going on we can question the idea that we carry our philosophy inside our 'selves.' Contact with each other in open, convivial, questioning engagement will reveal reality beyond personality. At this point we will have reached the apogee of philosophy, by collapsing one thing into another: Beauty *is* Good *is* Truth. Nothing is with or alongside, above or below; everything just is.

What happens when we consider an idea, a proposition, a proposal or an utterance of another person? The very process of thinking lies in the mental act of creating space in our mind for a new thought. What does this entail? Are we placing the newcomer, as it were, in the neatly-arranged order of our thoughts? Or are we (could we?) allow a measure of disturbance, a degree of upset, a 'paradigm-shift' in our head? Consideration or investigation is arguably a cornerstone in the activity of philosophy-making. The question before us is then: are we perhaps ultimately inconsiderate or thoughtless in our public and private discourse? And furthermore, can we say the same about philosophy?

As elegant as it may sound, 'thinking about thinking' takes us into ever more confusing thickets of confusion. It is difficult enough to conceive of thinking in the way just described. Yet we are immediately faced with a further challenge; that is to say, when we add the notion of meta-thinking to it. At this level of reflexive thinking the 'meta' is the core concept.

The 'meta' is a question of method. Inherent in philosophical method is an exploration of tensions between that which we are able to conceive at the moment and that which hasn't yet been conceived. Thinking generally starts with a hypothesis. But in order to drive a hypothesis forward we need to push it to the absolute. The tension between the conceived and not yet conceived is full of unreleased potential.

Nonetheless, no concept is on a par with reality. Rather, reality is a metaphor through which mind formulates or translates its intuitions about reality into its own language. Reality is so grand (like God) that it has to be translated into a set of constructs when we attempt to deal with the notion. To pitch mind against reality misses the point of philosophy. As we critique concepts they fall down or change, not into parts but into material from which we can build a more widely-embracing concept. To fall into dualism is a methodological error. The aim of method is to get us to reality. Yes, we can explore mind, but reality is the object.

A JOURNEY

The word method means 'going after the road' or 'looking out for the journey.' These quizzical constructions convey something that is not straight-forwardly logical; journeys ordinarily precede destinations. The relationship between journey and destination is of the same order as that between means and ends. The former takes us to the latter. However philosophy challenges the rules of logic in search of deeper truths. It asks for example if we can see the journey as the destination and the destination moreover as a projection of the journey itself. Can the notion of a journey towards a journey help us to understand what is awaiting us at the end of it all? Is there a hint here of the relationship of multiplicity to oneness or even an opportunity to abolish the two?

The first step is to sever the link between ends and means, along with associated notions such as causality, correlation and subsidiarity. It is precisely by freeing words from their syntactic allocation and allowing them to stand in their own right that the road from terminology to conceptualisation can begin. Language is now enriched to such an extent that a completely new and enhanced version of totality arises, which can only exist when everything reaches a full and independent existence as a mini-totality within itself. Thus instead of the idea of a means to an end we have the idea of everything as an end in itself. The distinction between outcome and effort, target and trajectory, output and input no longer holds. However, this is merely a beginning for, if we say the journey *is* the destination, we have still retained the underlying idea of destination. Further unfolding is required towards an idea that conveys the journey itself. The second step is to enter further into that aspect of the nature of things that is the 'within.' The subservient nature of relationships may well have eclipsed the truth and beauty of entities by creating, as it were, multi-varied relationships within the relationships themselves. Thirdly and most important of all, the means as an end in itself is followed by the seemingly unfathomable idea of the end as an ultimate means in its own right. This is to say that the end goal or Aristotelean *telos* is revealed as the Socratic dialogue reaches its crescendo.

The first part of the journey to the absolute of reality requires that we accept that reality is not definable. When attempts are made to define reality philosophy responds by collapsing the definition into its opposite. Reality and non-reality together promise greater potential insight than either promise alone. This is because reality includes its counterpart. Any method we use must be anchored by reality, not by the mind within it. For this reason philosophical method is not like any other method which is particular to a given area of study or practice. Science may be defined as an activity that follows its own methods; this is equally true of crafts. Their approach shapes the universe in an anthropomorphic image. Science has sometimes been accused of playing out the illusion that nature is an expansion of the human mind. People usually make their own lives the starting point of a journey to the absolute. Yet, to choose any particular way to travel forces us to neglect all other ways. In contrast, philosophy's journey is to the absolute; thus it deals with the whole of reality all at once. Method has to be up to the task of inclusion, which means it has to be anchored in reality, rather than being a mind-construct or a part within the whole. Method thus has no indefinite article; it is not one of many other methods but the idea of method. The nearest synonym is process, flow, movement or transmission (as through an empty vessel). Method is thus the nearest that we can initially approach to reality. Because reality is undefinable it opens up to method. The usual definition of method as a way of doing things that pins something down to this way or that diminishes method in the sense used here.

To state that philosophical method opens us up to reality is not hyperbole. Philosophy arose out of a sense that reality is obscured from us by the very faculty – mind – that we use to search for it. Other thought systems are aware of this. But philosophical method insists on utter transparency by questioning everything that it brings up. Its method is thus to think about the thinking that we so trusted in the first place. This method forces us to consider the nature of thinking itself, and then to reconsider it again and again. For it is in the nature of totalities (for which we may read: realities) to respond to a freeing (letting go, engaging and cultivating) of the mind. We cannot reconcile thought and being until this is complete.

The process of thinking (philosophical included) is not consistent; it slips this way and that, stumbling over short-cuts, slippages, assumptions, quick answers. It is tricky. Yet, nothing in the thinking process is wrong; it can only ever be incomplete. We can't see the whole picture. At some point we generally blame that which is not yet revealed as being wrong. Philosophy recognises that all problems are at bottom ones of method. It is not that life is complex, but rather that there is always more to things than we can see.

This is why philosophy is a journey of discovery. But not, as so many journeys are, with an end in view. It has no outcome or purpose. The Eleatic school of Greek thinkers were the first to realise that for us to be more real we must problematize our method of thinking. This doesn't mean showing a preference for one method over another, but of evolving a universal method that reflects all others. Philosophy is an end in itself *because* it focuses on the method of thinking rather than on this position or that conclusion; in other words it does not let the process of thinking ossify around any given point.

CHAPTER FOURTEEN - THE BODY AGAIN: WHAT CAN A BODY DO?

We must remember that there is no need to 'prove' that the body thinks. The Axial Age project was only a mind-construct, a thought-experiment - nothing was actually removed from the body. The key point is that the body is already in and of the world. The mind is only a concept. After pursuing the idea of a 'detached' mind for so long and having gaining an understanding of it, philosophy can terminate the experiment of appearing to separate it from the body. Knowledge of mind has become plentiful. (1) All the moves mentioned in the last chapter are ways of closing down this redundant idea. Only the body is left. Incidentally, mind's demise releases philosophy from the tyranny of epistemology, selfhood or personality, subjectivity in general, including psychology (the unconscious along with the conscious), ideology, materialism, and culture. We are well along the road to understanding how mind creates 'our' world, perceptions and emotions. But, for our purposes here, the 'I' is now left in a thoroughly pared-down state. Thus, we can return to the focus in the Introduction on the statement *that it is* (as opposed to *what it is*). *That it is* appertains to a primordial state of receptivity, femininity and acceptance. I express this primordial pared-down-ness in terms of a body possessing a capacity to transmit, contain and process thought. This body is the thing in itself. Like a holograph or monad it contains everything in microcosm. We can now assess the philosophical possibilities of this new territory

I

A starting point is the arch-monist (of one substance although two aspects) Spinoza. By putting God into Nature he presumably went as far as he believed the mood of contemporary religious society would allow. In effect he was saying that God doesn't exist, that everything is in the world. The point remains that he still made a category error by placing body and mind in two camps. Spinoza's thinking was ostensibly Cartesian; he set out to show that Descartes' mind-body split was false and he did this successfully. But Spinoza can still be accused of being a dualist: he countered Descartes' argument without removing it altogether. His solution is now our problem. He is in a long tradition descending from the extension-thought dualism of Aristotle. The contention put forward here is that there is only one category - the body - although it is possessed of many sub-categories. Rejection of Spinoza's monism in the 21st century might be explained by postmodernity's rejection of unity. But by bringing a dualist eye to bear on Spinoza's work many current thinkers see more than there is to see. Spinoza was a monist at heart; he found unity in the body.

He corrected Plato's mistake of putting reality outside the world. Yet, he was much more radical than that; he brought the focus of philosophy back to its method. Scepticism owes its central place in philosophy to its ability to falsify dichotomies. Thus, Spinoza realised that scepticism, *as a method*, lies at the heart of monism. Descartes had started with scepticism and had arrived at the Cogito, but crucially he did not thereby defeat scepticism; rather he integrated doubt into his thinking. This is the key point. Thought was thus enabled to overcome itself and - the key move – to strengthen its object of investigation. Thus, Spinoza doesn't turn his monist thinking into a seamless movement, into some sort of indeterminacy; nor on the other hand does he create mechanistic or deterministic positions or structures. He offers us a philosophical method with the power to open mind up to reality. He follows a sequence of thoughts that contains internal tensions: one thing doesn't quite move to the next thing. As a Gestalt move the present thought does not link up with the previous one in the sense of them being two discrete thoughts connecting laterally. Instead, the present thought *stems from* the previous one; it grows from or is inspired by it. In this process there is a muse at work. Reality is allowed to enter. The nature of this move leaves room for something unexpected to happen between the thoughts – something relational, stochastic, or unintended. In other words, *philosophically* the move from A to B is not to close a gap but to recognise its vibrancy. A doesn't lead to B; A is going nowhere. B arises out of its relationship to A. In terms of the fulcrum method outlined in Chapter Thirteen above this productive tension can be described as 'the third' or 'the in-between.' Something new occurs.

What this move tells us is that philosophy is not just about the actions of the mind. Something else is at work. Philosophy has dominantly been about the mind scrutinising itself, checking out the assumptions it makes. This is only a first move. What matters above everything else is that philosophy is reaching out to reality. It may be a laborious process, but this is made necessary because mind needs constantly to be aware of its own bifurcating tendency. Mind is used in philosophy as a self-critical, double move. At the outset, when reality is only a hypothesis, the philosophical exercise is solely mind-engaging-with-mind. As ever, the self is the danger; we must always have the courage to avoid becoming enamoured of the self. We can all sometimes feel nature calling us to emote, to love or to see beauty in things (indeed, artists can be said to be carried away in this regard and to inflame their imaginations). But philosophy is at heart sceptical. Doubting the mind is the key second move in philosophy.

Mind is after all only a hypothesis introduced by Plato in order to understand the relation of the body to the mind. Philosophy creates entities that seem to float above us for ever until we know what we are asking. Plato's method of teaching his students (and us) has been misunderstood. He can be said to be telling us – and this is a bold move – that we will understand body one day. In the meantime, we must first understand the idea of mind by treating it as if it is an entity in its own right. Before the 20th century the body was a corollary of the mind, reflected in the denial of the body in religion. The persistence of this dichotomous interpretation down to today has led us astray. Nonetheless, mind is being returned to the body in the 20th and 21st centuries, as Eagleton indicates. (2)

II

Those who have 'reclaimed' the body in the last century and a half did so in order that more reality could enter the body's force-field by avoiding the constraints erected by mind. Although these thinkers all hover on the brink of saying the body thinks, none categorically asserts it. (3) This doesn't reflect a lack of scientific nerve. In any case, the connection is immediate or all but so. When thought passes through the body it affects the immune system and can express itself in changes in body states. But more to the philosophical point, those thinkers did not seek to dwell on materiality. This would be a dualist move, for materiality is the opposite of immateriality. Instead, first and foremost, they sought to maintain discourse at the conceptual level and thereby stay faithful to Spinoza's method mentioned above. That is to say, they wanted to leave room for ideas to open up. Nonetheless, Nietzsche, Heidegger, Merleau-Ponty and Deleuze make it plain that the body *is* the world, in the way that the mind is not.

This is a fundamental reversal: it is no longer about the body being a corruptible fragment of physical nature. The body renders the world. This is the area to which I'm pointing: the body as a distinctive category-challenging, transformative holograph that tells us something about the world itself. Heidegger talks of human beings 'bodying forth' into the world. He adds,'[The body] is basically *not* inanimate matter but a domain of that nonobjectifiable, optically invisible opacity to receive-perceive the significance of what it encounters.' (4) Merlau-Ponty pondered what it meant for the body 'not to be matter, substance, or spirit, nor a representation of the mind.' 'Flesh' was for him the ultimate notion, an element of Being or '*a general thing*.' (5) On the other hand (according to Deleuze) Merleau-Ponty bound his thinking too tightly to subjectivity, the body's setting within an indivisible whole only tending to provide spiritual comfort. Things in the world evoke an echo in the body, and this creates a carnal formula of their presence. But his ontology of the flesh rests on a surface of sense-perceptions. If Merleau-Ponty was ultimately Apollonian, Deleuze's Dionysian 'meat' by contrast is dangerous. It is intense, vital and dynamic, responding unexpectedly to the unforeseen. It releases vital powers of rhythm, renders invisible and intensive forces fruitful, experiments with new compounds and alliances between forces, and opens up new forms of existence. But all this essaying into definitional territory is not the point. Their reluctance to give a verifiable definition of body left room for new questions to arise. In the way that ideas have historically ebbed and flowed between the extremes of Platonic otherworldliness and Aristotelean particularism the philosophers of the body found the particular in the world and vice versa.

III

What then does Spinoza's attempt to return the mind to the body tell us? Firstly, this was not a move bound within the two extremes of physicalism or materialism on the one hand or panpsychism on the other. It is a category move - to a much more complex view of the body. Using the nervous system the body maintains the internal milieu, modulating the amplitude of changes inside the organism with reference to outside influences. The range of possible internal states is geared to survival. The body is 'a haven of stability in the universe of change…' (6) Secondly, if we take his move further, the body has the power to anchor reflexive thought and allow more reality to enter the body's force field. Thought is now but one connector, sensor and responder, even if the largest, alongside the nervous, immune and other body systems.

What does this mean for philosophy and the lived life? It means that things manifest but do not ossify into a single form. Possibilities remain open. Mind settles down and relates closely to other properties of a thoroughly complex body. Thinking is now simple, mundane, unflustered, not drawn into panicking or excitation. We can live with more complexity because we have less need to impose rules on thinking. Only in this way can the 'I' engage fully with reality. Only in this way might thinking be able to address fully the nature and effects of the socio.

So, rather than the mind having evolved in search of itself a la Hegel, we can now posit body evolving in search of itself. Just as mind is a concept that helps us understand thinking, so also thought frees us to think that which isn't yet clear. Evolution progressed from bacteria to human beings, and some 2000 years ago consciousness was deemed to have separated from the body. Thinkers acclaimed what they saw as distinctive about the human being. Now however, we can complete Spinoza's radical move by allowing thinking to move through its primordial channel, the body.

CHAPTER FIFTEEN - WHOLENESS AND DAILY LIFE

So far I've set out to show how the body-mind dilemma can be put to rest. The way this might affect our lives is still an open question. However, in this chapter I suggest ten ways in which it might be possible for the ideas on preceding pages to affect daily living.

Firstly, the statement 'reality is everything there is' challenges all suppositions. Reality knows in advance of anything that mind can conceive and it sacrifices itself to mind. This means we have to make the first move. In order to live we can adopt Nietzsche's nostrum and stand tall. But this would solidify an even greater sense of self. Philosophy urges us to let go of the mind that validates the self. Indeed, people think philosophy offers itself as *something* – entity, thought system, solace - to which aspiring philosophers can cling. Yet, as a method, philosophy has to be enacted; it will not emerge by itself. The problem is mind. Perforce, mind has no given ethical dimension, no positive opposing a negative. In any case, because all is real, we can collapse any perceived negative into the positive, 'ought' into 'is.' The Platonic goodness is so total that to attempt to maximise it turns it into bad. Criminals can be seen as over- rather than under-ethical because they believe what their minds have told them. Yet, while a child is immersed in reality, an adult connects only to mind; the child questions outwards to the world, the adult questions within the self. Ethics has become such a top-heavy edifice, productive of ever-more sophisticated refinements and categories of behaviour and motivation it might already be a sub-division of psychology or science. Humans are not different from other animals beyond having a larger brain. There is no need for a separate system to administer relations between them. Pre-religious and pre-thinking societies did not see humans as different in kind. Reality can be left to sort out differences. Beyond any attempt we make to prove it is there or not, or to define in what sense, everything is real. If our mind tells us we struggle with reality we must abandon our mind. Things are not in us *per se*, they are in us because we are in reality. We need not gaze on life as if it is something in itself. Magnificence already describes life and us. There is no need to beautify it or us.

Secondly, we can follow Plato's advice to remember or recognise what is, even when we cannot configure it, and here we have arrived at the heart of philosophy. When we conceive of reality flowing in a primordial state, we can appreciate Plato's signal effort in harnessing the knowledge and ideas available up to his time. He made clear that virtues flow into each other, that passion (or energy) in any one part of the soul flows into other parts when the balance has slipped. Plato did a good packaging job. He realised that mind fragments reality, so he urged us to tessellate, fit things together again. His momentous contribution was to realise that philosophy was a tool. The fact that he could not take us further is explained by the scale of the unfinished work the Pre-Socratics had left behind. They talked only to each other in terms of the techniques known at the time. Plato integrated their conversation, but did not extend his work beyond them to include eastern theological questions of the time. Similarly, Plotinus put Plato's scattered or contradictory ideas into a package that said to us more than Plato could do. The job of reintegration of ideas goes on; the philosophical tools are available to un-staunch the flow and so re-engage with totality.

Ironically, reality is on our side in this endeavour; as Heraclitus pointed out, it is wise enough to unify multiplicity. We are not required to add some great insight or extra piece of knowledge. The story of 8 blind Indian men makes this plain. Their individual attempts to identify an elephant by reference to separate parts of it inevitably failed. But if we stand apart and watch all the blind men at once we can conceive of the whole elephant. There is no need for us to leap into action by adding a ninth contribution to this fragmented knowledge. Viewing the viewing (even as an exercise in deductive logic) and not making judgements on the basis of only one part puts us in touch with the whole.

Thirdly, when we obliterate the perceiver altogether, yet retain the perceiving faculty, we are engaging in reality. Put another way, the person we are listening to at any given moment is both an identifiable person and an idea standing for all reality external to us. In this way, Levinas tells us, the Other evokes me. It becomes clear that everything outside me is infinitely active if I hold my 'self' back. Reality continues to create me from one moment to the next. Calasso's call to let the gods return to our lives is a call for us to accept our immersion in reality. Communication between fragments (selves) and reality stumbles because of the partiality of our viewpoint; we can easily become one of the Indian blind men. The gods are glimpses of our part in reality. They return briefly: "I let go of myself; I wasn't myself then." In those moments we act as part of primordial reality, or from our id, as Freud described it. We first locate and identify this totality inside us. This experience can be described as appreciating that the universe contains more than we know. For example, someone (A) looks at a friend (B) and sees the friend; but the friend (B) looks at (A) and sees only herself (B). What has happened? We see ourselves in another, yet we also see other aspects of reality there, because reality (or God) is an open space. We tend of course to notice the features we are strongly disposed towards or against. Only however when we see the other as *everything* will we have let go of ourselves. One of the great flaws in Plato's thinking arose from his simultaneous attraction to out-and-out philosophy and his hesitation as he thought about where his intuitions might take him. He reached a junction and stalled; it was too much for him to create a full-blooded system of thought. A choice between thinking too much or very little paralysed him and he compromised. We can now free his ideas from compromise by realising that a middle path appears when antagonists see themselves in their opponent, and vice versa.

Fourthly, we can turn things on their head, as Socrates' questioning method was designed to do. Everyone invariably starts out by taking a position. We can obviate this move by reversing that position. Contrarians are able to replace content with process. In churches an oppositional stance is often avoided by getting the congregation to face God the unifier, not each other. Turning things on their head is a step towards reclaiming flow and harmony. So when for example, Buddhism says detach, we know that negotiating with the mind will fail once detachment ceases and mind returns. Rather, we can return all the way to reality. Plato took on all ideas, as did Aristotle; they did not argue with each other. A philosophical response is to integrate all available ideas.

Fifthly, the problems that emerge as a result of Descartes' split between the observer and the observed lie with the observer. Mind both observes and is the observed. Everyone has a place in the universe but they don't see themselves that way. When they are 'in the world' the mind is happy with itself with regard to other beings. But when it observes itself observing others it goes berserk. This is because it doesn't know how to observe itself. When looking outwards the mind's searching mistakes the search for the thing. Searching is productive if it is helped; otherwise it goes astray. Things go astray because the mind doesn't have enough knowledge. It cannot find the other. This is because the observer overdoes it, and so only meets another observer. A calm observer would leave the observed to emerge. It is already there in reality or in the world. When I leave the observed to themselves I let go of my doubt about the object. If I am still in doubt (about how the other takes me) I can ask the other. I will invariably discover it is all in my head.

Sixthly, the tricky question of detachment arises. How can we achieve this while remaining in the world? Systems of disengagement go back thousands of years to India, Israel, and to Christian monasteries. Societies have always deliberated between autonomy and participation – either as a mutually exclusive or as a balancing act, or as in any other juxtaposition of one and the other. Detachment has always been a means to an end, an attempt to encounter (or recreate) the world through the manoeuvres of the mind. The difficulty with it takes us back to the issue of recognition. Are we truly recognising things? Herein surely is the answer to liberation. We are all of and at one with the world, microcosms of the macrocosm. Thus to be free is to be become cognisant, aware if you wish, of the fact that what we wish to be liberated from is the very core of who we are. So, back to the question: can we be liberated from society while staying in the world? The answer is clearly yes, but it requires hard philosophical work - by raising questions, doubting values, screening theories and scrutinising language. Why yes? Firstly, both mind and the 'world' require conceptual analysis. Namely, that which seeks to liberate is but an echo of its core, and that which is seen as oppressive is but a representation of its kernel.

So, they both seek self-liberation within themselves, each adopting in their sweep the desire of the other, thus becoming entangled in an endless loop. Secondly, mind and the world are one and the same, intimately connected, directly recognised, both yearning to unite in an act of love. At heart (call it source, origin, beginning, telos or even God) they come from the same place, and they both know it. Thus, on the one hand a self-which-is-not-itself, feeling oppressed and seeking detachment, and on the other hand a world which is several times removed from the way it is. Both are engaged in seduction, temptation, immersion, repulsion. Isn't it a kind of comedy act?

Seventhly, the interpersonal has arisen as a step-change in our engagement with reality. Yet it might be that the interpersonal simply emerges as central to psychology, as a version of the notion of other 'minds.' The little gaps between minds and understanding thereof are what are missing in our grasp of oneself and reality. Time will tell whether relationship, friendship, fraternity or the in-between will ever emerge as a central philosophical concept. Friendship can be placed within philosophy as a concept. It is possible to survey one's inner soul with wonder rather than trepidation and then to seek to do the same with others. I become friends with those who by default didn't abandon me. Maybe the default position is all there is, the road less travelled. There's a lot to be said for us being our own worst enemies, and one way of rectifying this is to make allowance for that which is not immediately apparent. We do not need to act as an agent of choice but rather to submit to the flow, encounter in it the surprising and unexpected. Hence we find ourselves with strange bedfellows – and do not flinch from them.

The idea of relationship is embedded in connectivity, in attraction, in love. It hints at how open we are, how prone to interact, how dependent on feedback, the degree to which we thrive on encounter. It's not unthinkable that sometime in the future the notion of mind will be addressed through the lens of relationship. As far as can be seen at the moment it is not the individual who fails but the network, system or web. As we strive for liberation we have to remove one chain after another standing in the way of authenticity. Most people seem to carry on their backs the cross of others, which is not theirs to carry. Thus, as ever, relationship is paradoxical. That is, in order to achieve it one has to recognise the range of connections already there and standing in the way. The issue is not that selfhood prevents relationship; rather, that unrecognised relationships (attachments), block the way for authentic ones.

Eighthly, we can make use of Socratic irony and playfulness. Of course we cannot *know* reality because we are immersed in it. Yet, we have to address the conundrum that is mind. It is the only tool we have that is capable both of clearing away the debris that mind itself has created and also of addressing mind's own claim to stand in place of reality. Only when this job is done can we go ahead and kill mind. One such response to the conundrum is the modern equivalent of Socratic irony and playfulness – a thought-experiment. We usually claim that mind looks at something. If we reverse the process and make mind the object then philosophy can look at it, as if under a microscope. Mind is no longer a personal experience; rather mind has been conceived by concepts. Philosophy is now a fulcrum – it is neither mind nor reality but rather it looks at both. It is an invitation to transcend everything as a means to an end. As such it becomes an end in itself. Thus, with Socratic irony philosophy emerges as the end that justifies the means that is already there to justify the end. Thus philosophy begins to conceive of us: we change from subject to object. The capacity of philosophy to transfigure our thinking in these ways throws a light on the lateral (and split) thinking we usually fall back on.

Ninthly, we can incorporate the margins rather than stick to Aristotle's mean. Mysticism presents itself as just such a counterintuitive yet fruitful area of investigation. When meta-thinking seems the only step open to philosophers they usually stop and claim that going any further would be to enter the realm of mysticism. For example we can glimpse the socio in Spinoza's claim that adequate thinking will take us to joy. This is a dichotomous statement that assumes that deeper thinking will take us into the abyss. Need this be so?

Finally, a response to the above question is to notice what happens in the famous Socratic encounter. We have not yet brought to completion Socrates' attempt to free entities from a symbiotic, cloying embrace of each other. Philosophical method and Socratic questioning remove the gaze from an object and turn it back on the gazer. Now untold forces are released. As the investigator emerges from behind the apparatus of the investigation, or the problem reorients itself as it is problematized, constraints on thinking will become clearer. We can begin to see that philosophy has succumbed to the grip of its disciples; and realise that much of extant philosophical method is actually unreconstructed science, political philosophy or sociology, which in the terms we have used, is first-level thinking. It fails to look at itself in the act of thinking.

CONCLUSION

The bird in TS Eliot tells us humankind cannot bear very much reality. Yet the unique achievements of the early Greeks have been attributed to their having borne much more reality than most human beings before or since (1). The lack of public attention hitherto paid to reality suggests a widespread preparedness to settle for what the mind tells us. Yet, this is to accept the world as matrix. So much of popular culture is telling us what serious thinking is veering away from. Does this suggest that people at large are in fact more in touch with the early Greek spirit of exploration than 'official' thinkers? Baudrillard's nightmare has come true: reality has disappeared before our very eyes. Something more real than the real, a virtual or 'hyperreal' has taken its place.

I have placed two concepts – the body and the socio – at the heart of this book. They deserve the closest of philosophical scrutiny in the future. Arguably modern ills and philosophy's up-rootedness from life can be explained by reference to a failure to understand the mutual relationship between the body and the socio. The body seems immune to the power of the socio. It is a conduit through which thinking can move freely when the grip of mind is broken. It is thus a foundation which sustains a life free of anxiety and makes possible an exploration of the socio unencumbered by presuppositions. By going beyond Spinoza to a concept of a body as a conduit for thought I have presented a case for a less driven, clever, compensatory way of life. Immanent and Dionysian, this way of connecting is clean and direct. I take this to lie behind the Axial Age thinkers' original desire to separate mind from body as the first step towards understanding what it means for human beings to be free.

I've made many references to the early Greeks. They didn't seek to understand reality; instead their open minds allowed them to stay immersed in it without panicking or wondering if they would have to pay a price for their openness. Admittedly they lived 'when the world was young,' but they were prepared to see the world as a new place each day; to face new ideas or interpretations without trepidation; and, as JB Bury put it, they were accustomed 'to take little and give much.' (2)

Equally, the threat of savagery was never distant from the genius of the Greeks. They faced raw reality without trepidation. This is why the philosophical project might seem harsh. It asks us to test our own life against reality in the awareness there is no other test, head held high when others panic. It tells us reality is bigger than love; even parenting must make allowance for it. Yes, we are there for our children, partners and friends, but we can only be there fully when we are real. Then we are there in an entirely different way. We can let go of partial or hesitant responses. No longer need we seek amelioration or turn to sentimentality, no longer offer tiredness or vulnerability as a reason to withdraw or prevaricate. No longer must we measure life by our ability to contain anxiety. No longer have we to see philosophy as consolation for the trials and tribulations of life a la Boethius or in recent times de Botton and others. Further, loving relationship, the modern divinity, can now be seen as the original sin, for mind has seeped into every corner, pulling the socio in its train. Husband and wife must always adopt rigid roles; marriage has to be lived as a series of rituals. A universe without philosophy would not allow us to conceive of reality. And yet being real is I aver the only approach that delivers.

I have pointed to mind as the chief culprit. It has long been seen as a defence against reality. The power of the mind to create a self that separates from humankind has fascinated humankind. It reverberates down from the Greek myths in which Odysseus and his wife Penelope's strong sense of self caused them to lead solitary lives, 'with hearts of iron,' (3) to the Freudian idea of psychopathy. And yet, despite the groundwork of the Greeks, Descartes' idea of the Cogito has bred a fascination with subjectivity down to this day. Spinoza pointed to the connectedness of everything, but even now monism has not loosened the grip of subjectivity within the philosophical canon. Indeed the innumerable works on theories of mind, subjectivity and phenomenology are testament to the hold exerted by mind and its attendant belief in self and agency.

Yet, my intention was never to propose a duel between mind and the socio on one side and reality and the body on the other. Rather it was to plead for reality to be seen apropos everything - culture, knowledge, language, ethics, aesthetics, and even philosophical method itself; indeed anything that claims separate status or authority. Inevitably, every time we seek to talk about something we seem to leave something else out. But philosophy says no, include everything, we can keep going beyond limitation. In other words, challenge Kant's and Wittgenstein's conclusions! Reality is open to me in its entirety regardless of Kant's limits of reason; the limits of my language are not, as Wittgenstein claims, the limits of my world.

The philosophical invitation is to address everything as real. As a move in this direction it says that everything includes its counterpart. Knowledge will say of that which we know that 'it is ok.' But reality is not the study of what is definable. It even challenges the idea of reality. In this spirit it includes all such 'other sides' as the unreal. Philosophy, like infinity, is elastic; it stretches to encompass all things beyond any delineation. Socrates and Plato envisaged all knowledge to be at an end, while the knower remains. They brought mind to the centre of things and then removed it. This is the end of the road. Mind cedes to reality and finally accepts its harmonious place in the universe.

I set out moreover to show that when we refer to thinking we are referring to the body as the site through which thought passes. Accordingly, once we loosen the grip of mind we are free to contemplate a bigger threat than mind ever presented. I argue that the body is not seduced by the socio. The thorough-going questioning that characterises metaphysics and philosophical method is akin to the processes that occur when mind is anchored in the body. This can one day lead to a greater understanding of this double-headed monster. For, aside from its veritable manipulation of reality, the socio has created so much that we appreciate, from cathedrals to hospitals, that it would be self-harming in the extreme to dismiss it.

But, beyond issues of body or socio, I have set out to extend Rosenzweig's 'New Thinking.' His approach takes us beyond the edifice-building of German Idealism into a world that is not fixated on a human point of view or on the minutiae of the canon. Rosenzweig was at one with Socrates and Martin Buber in seeing that new thought emerges from within encounters, building on a pre-existing connectivity that allows us to take our place in the world without anxiety.

Philosophy invites us to wonderment. It does not require that we regulate our lives or measure them against a moral yardstick. As Bernard-Henri Levy asks (with regard to Judaism), 'what can one say about those texts by Levinas that also flirt with atheism and tell us Judaism is not a way of seeing but a way of living; that what's at stake is transmission rather than revelation, and that it[']s great[,] it[']s real concern is man's relationship, not with God but with his fellow man.'(4) Levy sees people as vessels through which things pass – thoughts, feelings, intuitions, intimations; we are connected with everything. If we allow ourselves to be receptive then reality will reach out to us. Wonderment (Greek: *theoria*) is the wondering contemplation of the divine in which, as Michael Foster points out: 'mystery is not dispelled but is more fully revealed.' (5) We do not need to do anything other than, as Spinoza tells us, appreciate life under the aspect of eternity.

Thus we are as real as anything, warts and all, and our task is not to weed or trim or clean up. Rather, our task is to stand up and account for ourselves, courageously face up to our energies, not fuss over this aspect or the other; rise above guilt or shame and accept the intrinsic, the immanent, potential and the possible in us, in others, and in all else, not merely as heading towards health, wellbeing, happiness, fulfilment or actualisation, or even Telos, but the sensation – unequalled and unparalleled - of being who we are as an embodiment, indeed as a reintegration of all that can be. For, when we accept ourselves as whole, those aspects we can't presently accept will disappear and naturally return where they belong, where they came from. To worry about ourselves is superfluous from a philosophical standpoint, even though it may not be so through other prisms or perspectives. We are a product of our continuing attempt not to be ourselves, augmented and re-enforced albeit inadvertently by childhood, parents and countless others. So, liberation is the ability to recognise the whole, the courage and stamina to resist onslaughts from in and outside, regarding petty aspects of this or that. It requires the skill to ask questions about the very questions we ask. Liberation asks us not to fall back on answers and solutions and ready-made theories; rather, above all else, to see ourselves as an integral part of reality, not an observer separate from it.

ENDNOTES

Introduction

(1) Of these names perhaps the least known today is Franz Rosenzweig. See Franz Rosenzweig, 'The New Thinking,' in Alan Udoff and Barbara E Galli (eds.) *Franz Rosenzweig's 'The New Thinking'* (1925; Syracuse NY, Syracuse University Press, 1999) which is a delayed introduction to Franz Rosenzweig, *The Star of Redemption* (1921; Madison and London, Wisconsin University Press, 2005). Also see Martin Buber, *I and Thou* (Trans. Ronald Gregor Smith, New York, Scribner, 2000); Ivan Illich, *Tools for Conviviality* (London and New York, Marion Boyers, 2009 edition); Irving Yalom, *The Schopenhauer Cure* (New York, HarperCollins, 2005 edition).

(2) Gilles Deleuze, *Nietzsche and Philosophy* (London and New York, Continuum, 1986) p 36.

(3) Gilbert Murray, 'The Value of Greece to the Future of the World,' in R W Livingstone (ed.) *The Legacy of Greece* (London, Clarendon *Press 1921;* Oxford, Oxford University Press, 1969

edition) p 17. Thomas Nagel expressed a wish to be part of reality rather than an observer of it. 'How can one bring into one's individual life a recognition of one's relation to the universe as a whole, whatever that is…? Is there a way to live in harmony with the universe, and not just in it?' Quoted in Galen Strawson, 'Religion as Sin,' *London Review of Books* (Vol 33, No 11, 2 June 2011).

(4) Wilfred Sellars's claim that the given is a myth relies on arguments drawn from analytic philosophy and theory of mind. His appeal to epistemology, science and semantics reveals a fascination with what mind claims or creates rather than with what reality presents. See Willem A deVries and Timm Triplett (eds.) *Knowledge, Mind and the Given: Reading Wilfred Sellar's 'Empiricism and the Philosophy of Mind,'* (Indianapolis, Hackett Publishing, 2000).

(5) AW Moore, *The Evolution of Modern Metaphysics: Making Sense of Things* (New York, Cambridge University Press, 2013 edition).

(6) "The more we know of the brain, the less it looks like a device for creating consciousness: it's just a big collection of biological cells and a blur of electrical activity – all machine and no ghost.' Colin McGinn, 'All Machine and No Ghost?' *New Statesman,* 20 February 2012, p 43. An extensive literature on body-mind issues has grown in recent times. See for example Gilbert Ryle, *The Concept of Mind* (London, Penguin, 1949); Richard Rorty, *Philosophy and the Mirror of Nature* ((Oxford, Blackwell, 1980); Thomas Nagel, *The View from Nowhere* (New York, Oxford University Press, 1989 edition); Daniel Dennett, *Consciousness Explained* (London, Penguin, 1993 edition); Antonio Damasio, *Descartes' Error*: *Emotion, Reason and The Human* Brain (London, Vintage, 2006); Colin McGinn, *The Mysterious Flame: Conscious Minds in a Material World* (New York, Basic Books, 1999); Nick Chater, *The Mind is Flat: The Illusion of Mental Depth and the Improvised Mind ((London, Allen Lane,* 2018).

(7) Gilles Deleuze and Felix Guattari, *Anti-Oedipus: Capitalism and Schizophrenia* (trans. Robert Hurley, Mark Seem and

Helen R Lane, London and New York, Continuum 1972; 2004 edition) p 45. The body has been taken to the centre of cognitive science but only to sustain a materialist argument. See George Lakoff and Mark Johnson, *Philosophy in the Flesh: The Embodied Mind and its Challenge to Western Thought* (New York Basic Books, 1999). For the persistent influence of Kant see Anthony Morgan (ed.) *The Kantian Catastrophe? Conversations on Finitude and the Limits of Philosophy* (Newcastle upon Tyne, Bigg Books, 2017).

(8) Gilles Deleuze, *Cinema II: The Time-Image* (London, Bloomsbury, 2013 edition) p 195.

Chapter One: Philosophy.

(1) In Heidegger's usage, logos and phusis were one.

(2) Moore, *Evolution of Modern Metaphysics,* p 605.

(3) Roberto Calasso, *The Marriage of Cadmus and Harmony* (New York, Alfred E Knopf, 1993) p 387.

(4) There is no doubt that the lived life can be an unequal struggle: mental health and loneliness are presently (2018) rising up the British Government's agenda. Press Release 7 January 2018, Prime Minister's Office; 'Theresa May unveils biggest shake up of mental health policies in 30 years,' *The Telegraph*, 7 May 2017.

(5) Lars Iyer, 'Real philosophers have a burning sense of vocation,' *theguardian.com*. 24 November 2015.

Chapter Two: Reality is All There Is.

(1) Moore, *Evolution of Modern Metaphysics*, p 5. But his emphasis on the sense of things leads him to include meaning, purpose, explanation, something to live for, and understanding how things work. These are matters that arise from the vantage-point of the subject, but are not so when we consider reality as the nature of all things.

(2) Roughly 800-200 BCE. Karen Armstrong says that all the thought systems that grew then agreed that life

contained a transcendent element that was essential to the development of full human beings. Karen Armstrong, *A History of God (London, Vintage, 1999 edition)* pp 37, 51.

(3) Hugh Lloyd-Jones, *The Justice of Zeus* (Berkeley and London, University of California Press, 1973 ed.) p 164.

Chapter Three: The Body.

(1) I lean on Colin McGinn, 'All Machine and No Ghost?' *New Statesman,* Philosophical Special, 20 February (2012) in this section.

(2) Terry Eagleton, *Materialism* (New Haven and London, Yale University Press, 2016); Antonio Damasio, *Looking for Spinoza* (London, Vintage, 2004).

(3) Neuroscience focuses on the brain as an organ that has become elevated to an autonomous status. Different from all other organs, it has come to be seen as different in kind, as a controller of mind.

(4) See the treatment of this idea in Deleuze and Guattari, *Anti-Oedipus;* Maurice Merleau-Ponty, *The Visible and the Invisible* (Ed. Claude Lefort; Trans.

Alphonso Lingis; Evanston, Northwestern University Press, 1968).

(5) Terry Eagleton thinks so; see Eagleton, *Materialism*, p 151.

(6) Damasio, *Looking for Spinoza,* especially Chapter 5.

Chapter Four: Philosophy and Human Wellbeing.

(1) Rosenzweig, *Star of Redemption, p 190.*

Chapter Five: Mind and Philosophy.

(1) The fulcrum method involves letting go of a sense of self such that the mind is totally open to all that enters it.

(2) As opposed to repetitious, learned or structured thought which starts in opposition or comparison to something else.

(3) Foucault excoriates those who 'refuse to think without immediately thinking that it is man who is thinking.' Michel Foucault, *The Order of Things* (Abingdon, Routledge Classics, 2002 edition) p 373.

(4) Gary Gutting, *Thinking the Impossible: French Philosophy Since 1960* (Oxford, Oxford University Press, 2011) pp 120-121. See also Hilary Putnam, *Jewish Philosophy as a Guide to Life* (Bloomington and Indianapolis, Indiana University Press, 2008) especially Chapter 4. Putnam sees the idea of the Other as passing down a line of Jewish philosophy that included Franz Rosenzweig.

Chapter Six: The Death of God and the Rise of Mind.

(1) Even though Heidegger muddies the waters by placing the concept of ontology in the realm of the self.

Chapter Nine: The Socio: Aggregation and the Nature of Entities.

(1) Spinoza claimed that 'when a number of bodies…form close contact with one another through the pressure of other bodies upon them, or if they are moving…so as to preserve an unvarying relation among themselves, these bodies are said to be united with one another and all together to form one body or

individual thing.' An analysis of the idea of a journey and the above quotation are in Moore, *Metaphysics, pp* 52, 599-600.

(2) The literature on we-intentions and plural agency from Searle to Ludwig focuses on individualistic accounts of group agency, motivation, intentions and behaviour, with a leaning towards institutional and corporate states and processes, and towards 'social reality.'

(3) Rosenzweig, *Star of Redemption,* pp *53,* 55-58.

(4) *Ibid.,* p 58.

(5) CS Lewis, *The Four Loves* (London, HarperCollins 2002 edition) Chapters 4 and 5.

Chapter Ten: Philosophy Penetrated.

(1) Moore, *Evolution of Modern Metaphysics,* p 6. The large number of publications on moral philosophy might convince a disinterested bystander that moral philosophy *comprises* philosophy as a whole. Not so; its popularity indicates a predilection to follow the zeitgeist. Moreover, these publications reveal an uncritical tendency to find their intellectual anchor within their own sub-division of philosophy rather than in reality, in a fragment of the whole, oblivious to the attempts of metaphysics to connect up all the dots and so provide an underpinning for everything.

Chapter Eleven: Philosophy Penetrated (Cont'd).

(1) Moore, *Evolution of Modern Metaphysics,* p 6.

(2) Martin Heidegger, *Basic Writings* (Ed. David Farrell Krell; London and New York, Routledge, 2011 edition) pp 56-57.

(3) G. Santayana, *The Realm of Essence,* (London, Constable, 1928) p 116, quoted in F M Cornford, *The Unwritten Philosophy and Other Essays,* ed. WKC

Guthrie (Cambridge, Cambridge University Press, 1950) pp 76-77.

Chapter Twelve: Philosophy Resurgent: Metaphysics.

(1) AW Moore, 'Carving at the Joints,' *London Review of Books,* Vol 34, No 16, 30 August 2012.

(2) Moore, *Metaphysics*, p 605.

Chapter Thirteen: Philosophy Resurgent: Method.

(1) Archimedes is believed to have remarked; 'Give me a place to stand on and a lever long enough and I will move the world.' The idea of a fulcrum is used here to mean that thinking to the universal allows particularities and dichotomies to be seen as integral and not central to the world.

(2) The other two are: How do we know anything? and What is a good life?

(3) This argument is elaborated in Franz Rosenzweig, '"Germ

Cell" of *The Star of Redemption,'* in Alan Udoff and Barbara E Galli (eds.) *Franz Rosenzweig's 'The New Thinking' (Syracuse, Syracuse University Press,* 1999).

Chapter Fourteen: The Body Again

(1) Daniel C Dennett, *Consciousness Explained* (London, Penguin, 1993 edition); Lisa Feldman Barrett, *How Emotions are Made: The Secret Life of the Brain* (London, Pan Books, 2018 edition); Nick Chater, *The Mind is Flat: The Illusion of Mental Depth and The Improvised Mind* (London, Allen Lane, 2018)

(2) Terry Eagleton, *Materialism,* Chapter Two.

(3) I make no reference to developments in cognitive science because the thinking is dualistic. They claim that structured thinking arises from the biological make-up of human beings. There is no appreciation that materialism is one side of a divide, immaterialism being the other. It follows from this dualism that human beings are neural beings in

which thinking in the body is structured. I am pointing to the body as an anchor of thought that frees it from structures. See George Lakoff and Mark Johnson, *Philosophy in the Flesh: The Embodied Mind and its Challenge to Western Thought* (New York, Basic Books, 1999).

(4) Quoted in Jesus Adrian Escudero, 'Heidegger and the Hermeneutics of the Body,' *International Journal of Gender and Women's Studies* (online), June 2015, Vol 3, No 1, pp 16-25. Escudero comments: 'The body has a tacit knowledge of itself in the world. It is already woven into its environment, is immersed in a phenomenological fields of action that it understands before the inside-outside, subject-object distinction. This tacit knowledge precedes our objective consciousness of things.' (p 18)

(5) Deleuze, *Cinema II,* p 195; Merleau-Ponty, *The Visible and the Invisible,* pp 139-147. See also Daniela Voss, 'The Philosophical Concept of Meat and Flesh: Deleuze and Merleau-Ponty,' *Parrhesia* (No. 18, 2013).

(6) Antonio Damasio, *The Feeling Of What Happens: Body, Emotion and the Making of Consciousness* (London, Vintage, 2000) p 142.

Conclusion

(1) Roger Scruton suggests the members of the Symposium watered their wine for this reason. Roger Scruton, 'Here's to Bacchus,' *New Statesman,* 15 March 2004; special supplement, 'One Too Many,' pp xxvi-xxvii.

(2) Hugh Lloyd-Jones, *Justice of Zeus,* p 164; Murray in Livingstone, *Legacy of Greece,* p 17.

(3) Calasso, *Marriage of Cadmus and Harmony,* pp 373-74.

(4) Michel Houellebecq and Bernard-Henri Levy, *Public Enemies* (London, Atlantic Books, 2001) p 187.

(5) Foster, *Mystery and Philosophy,* pp 34, 37 f2.

WORKS REFERRED TO IN THE TEXT

Karen Armstrong, *A History of God* (London, Vintage, 1999 edition).

Lisa Feldman Barrett, *How Emotions are Made: The Secret Life of the Brain* (London, Pan Books, 2018).

Alain de Botton, *The Consolations of Philosophy* (London, Penguin, 2001 edition).

Nick Chater, *The Mind is Flat: The Illusion of Mental Depth and the Improvised Mind* (London, Allen Lane, 2018).

Roberto Calasso, *The Marriage of Cadmus and Harmony* (New York, Alfred A Knopf, 1993).

FW Cornford, *The Unwritten Philosophy and Other Essays* ed. WKC Guthrie (Cambridge, Cambridge University Press, 1950).

Antonio Damasio, *The Feeling of What Happens: Body, Emotion and the Making of Consciousness* (London, Vintage, 2000).

Looking for Spinoza (London, Vintage, 2004).

Descartes' Error (London, Vintage, 2006).

Gilles Deleuze and Felix Guatteri *Anti-Oedipus: Capitalism and Schizophrenia* (trans,

Robert Hurley, Mark Seen and Helen S Lane, London and New York, 1972; Continuum 2004).

Gilles Deleuze, *Cinema II: The Time-Image* (London, Bloomsbury, 2013).

Nietzsche and Philosophy (London and New York, Continuum, 1986).

Willem deVries and Timm Triplett, *Knowledge, Mind and the Given: Reading Wilfred Sellars's 'Empiricism and the Philosophy of Mind,'* (Indianapolis, Hackett Publishing, 2000).

Daniel Dennett, *Consciousness Explained* (London, Penguin, 1993).

Terry Eagleton, *Materialism* (New Haven and London, Yale University Press, 2010).

Jesus Adrian Escudo, 'Heidegger and the Hermeneutics of the Body,' *International Journal of Gender and Women's Studies,* (online, Vol 3, No 1, 2015).

Jules Evans, *Philosophy For Life and Other Dangerous Situations* (London, Rider Books, 2013 edition).

Michael B Foster, *Mystery and Philosophy* (London, SCM Press, 1957).

Michel Foucault, *The Order of Things* (Abingdon Oxon, Routledge Classics, 2002 edition).

John Gray, *Straw Dogs: Thoughts on Humans and Other Animals* (London, Granta, 2002) pp 78, 81.

Martin Heidegger, *Basic Writings* (Edited by David Farrell Krell) (Routledge, London, 2011 edition).

Michel Houellebecq, *Atomised* (London, Vintage Books, 2001 edition).

Michel Houellebecq and Bernard-Henri Levy, *Public Enemies* (London, Atlantic Books, 2001).

Ivan Illich, *Tools for Conviviality* (London, Marion Boyars, 2009).

Lars Iyer, 'Real philosophers have a burning sense of vocation,' *theguardian.com,* 24 November 2015.

Gary Gutting, *Thinking the Impossible: French Philosophy since 1960,* (Oxford, Oxford University Press, 2011).

CS Lewis, *The Four Loves* (London, HarperCollins, 2002 edition).

R W Livingstone (ed.) *The Legacy of Greece* (London, Clarendon Press 1921; Oxford, Oxford University Press, 1969 edition).

George Lakoff and Mark Johnson, *Philosophy in the Flesh: The Embodied Mind and its Challenge to Western Thought* (New York, Basic Books, 1999).

Hugh Lloyd-Jones, *The Justice of Zeus* (Berkeley, Los Angeles and London, University of California Press, 1975 edition).

Kirk Ludwig, *From Individual to Plural Agency: Collective Action;* Vol 1 (Oxford, Oxford University Press, 2016).

Colin McGinn, 'All Machine and No Ghost?' *New Statesman,* 20 February 2012.

Colin McGinn, *The Mysterious Flame: Conscious Minds in a Material World* (New York, Basic Books, 1999).

Maurice Merleau-Ponty, *The Visible and the Invisible* (Ed. Claude Lefort; trans. Alphonso Lingis, Evanston Ill, Northwestern University Press, 1987).

A W Moore, *The Evolution of Modern Metaphysics: Making Sense of Things* (New York; Cambridge University Press, 2013 edition)

Anthony Morgan (ed.) *The Kantian Catastrophe? Conversations on Finitude and the Limits of Philosophy* (Newcastle upon Tyne, Bigg Books, 2017)

Gilbert Murray, 'The Value of Greece to the Future of the World, ' in RW Livingstone (ed.) *The Legacy of Greece,* above.

Thomas Nagel, *The View from Nowhere* (New York, Oxford University Press, 1989 edition).

Hilary Putnam, *Jewish Philosophy as a Guide to Life: Rosenzweig, Buber, Levinas, Wittgenstein* (Bloomington IN, Indiana University Press, 2008)

Richard Rorty, *Philosophy and the Mirror of Nature* (Oxford, Basil Blackwell, 1980).

Franz Rosenzweig, '"Germ Cell" of *The Star of Redemption'* and 'The New Thinking' in Alan Udoff and Barbara E Galli (eds.) *Franz Rosenzweig's 'The New Thinking'* (1925; Syracuse NY, Syracuse University Press, 1999).

Franz Rozenzweig, *The Star of Redemption* (1921; Syracuse NY, Syracuse University Press, 2005).

Gilbert Ryle, *The Concept of Mind* (London, Penguin, 1949).

G. Santayana, *The Realm of Essence* (London, Constable, 1928).

Benedict de Spinoza, *Ethics* (London, Penguin, 1994).

Roger Scruton, 'Here's to Bacchus,' *New Statesman* (15 March 2004, Special Supplement: One Too Many, pp xxvi-xxvii).

Daniela Voss, 'The Philosophical Concept of Meat and Flesh: Deleuze and Merleau-Ponty,'*Parrhesia (No 18, 2013).*

Irvin Yalom, *The Schopenhauer Cure* (New York, HarperCollins, 2005 edition).

GLOSSARY

ABSOLUTE (THE) is a concept with theological connotations. It conveys that which is not bounded by or conditional on anything else. It can stand for the ground of being or the unity of reality.

APORIA is a term that denotes the space that appears when fixed ideas collapse under assiduous interrogation. New ideas can grow in this space. *Aporia* dislodges mind (fixed ideas) after it has come to dominate thinking. Mind then cedes its position and finds its place in the harmony of the universe.

A PRIORI (An) is a supposition about a state of being that subsists before I think about it. It makes necessary that I acknowledge the always-already nature of reality and the subjective nature of mind.

FULCRUM PHILOSOPHY is another term for metaphysics. It derives from Archimedes' claim that, if he could find ground firm enough and a piece of wood long enough to rest on a fulcrum, a small object at one end could balance the world at the other. This analogy conveys a sense that the world can be comprehended by conceptualising it; that by stepping far enough away from the world in thought one encompasses the whole.

HYPOTHESIS (An) is the speculative initiation of an idea, question or solution. It may contain elements of what is already known but, by its nature, must also include what is not known in order for new ground to be opened up.

METAPHYSICS is a form of enquiry that asks about the nature of things. As such it grounds philosophical thinking and underpins all branches of philosophy.

MIND (THE) is a concept that evolved to denote the structuring propensity of cognitive powers. By imposing definition and order upon thought it blocks the free movement of thought. Because it imposes closure in this way I call it non-thinking. Mind is not a capacity inherent in the world. It arises out of a human predilection for thought to be made personal or subjective. Mind can be made innocuous once it is anchored in the body, that is to say, in the world.

OTHER (THE) is a concept associated with Emmanuel Levinas. He claimed the Other stands outside one's mental construction of the world. Whether as an actual person or something that is beyond rational recognition, one's encounter with the Other breaks through the categories of thought that govern the way one lives. Levinas insists that the Other is crucial for one to be a person, both as a moral agent and as a reflective, rational being.

PROCESS occurs when movement of thought is unimpeded. It is similar to *aporia* (above) which creates a space in which new ideas can grow. Process is blocked when the mind imposes structures on to thinking.

REALITY is everything there is. It does not succumb to duality. It contains all dualities without itself being split.

SOCIO (THE) is a totality or a force that acts as a simulacrum of totality that rivals reality.

THOUGHT arises out of the reflective capacity inherent in the world. It is transmitted by the human body which is part of the world. Its freedom of movement is preserved when it is not constrained by the mind

TOTALITY see Reality above.

TRUTH is the potential that opens when self is abandoned, or alternatively when one side of a dichotomy can be conceived of as including the other side.

UNIVERSE see Reality above.

WORLD see Reality above

BIOGRAPHICAL NOTE.

Roy Sturgess was a lecturer in economic history at universities in England, Scotland and the United States. He took up philosophy in retirement, eventually becoming chair of a local society. He sees philosophy - searching for truth - as the questioning of all opinions. He remains active in a number of groups that explore philosophy as a conversation or as a Socratic dialogue.

INDEX

www.ingramcontent.com/pod-product-compliance
Ingram Content Group UK Ltd.
Pitfield, Milton Keynes, MK11 3LW, UK
UKHW020223250726
13967UKWH00001B/153

9 781999 308612